A PHOTOGRAPHIC HISTORY OF THE
ORIENT LINE

A PHOTOGRAPHIC HISTORY OF THE
ORIENT LINE

CHRIS FRAME, RACHELLE CROSS, ROB HENDERSON AND DOUG CREMER

The
History
Press

To the Orient Line, its founders and all those
who cherish its memory.

First published 2018

The History Press
The Mill, Brimscombe Port
Stroud, Gloucestershire, GL5 2QG
www.thehistorypress.co.uk

British Library Cataloguing in Publication Data.
A catalogue record for this book is available from the British Library.

ISBN 978 0 7509 6992 5

Typesetting and origination by The History Press
Printed and bound in India by Thomson Press India Ltd

Front cover: Surrounded by tugs and an
assortment of craft *Oriana* is welcomed into
Sydney on her maiden voyage 30 December
1960. (Henderson/Cremer collection ref. 6034)
Back cover: Orsova departing Melbourne for
the final time. (Henderson/Cremer Collection,
ref. 10544)
Frontispiece: *Orion* at Naples. (Henderson/
Cremer collection ref. OH6112)
Half-title page: *Orford* at Venice. (Henderson/
Cremer collection ref. OH11914)
Title page: *Orion* departing Sydney. (Henderson/
Cremer collection ref. 10021)

CONTENTS

Acknowledgements   6

Foreword by Commodore Christopher Rynd   7

Introduction   9

Salvaging History   13

1   Origins   15

2   Early History of The Orient Steam Navigation Company   23

3   Government Contracts   43

4   Into the Future   51

5   The Break Up   66

6   The Great Requisition   80

7   Rebuilding the Fleet   90

8   The Great Depression   105

9   A Second Global War   126

10   Post-War Rebuilding   139

11   P&O – Orient Line   155

12   The End of Orient   164

     Appendix 1: Orient Line of Clipper Ships   193

     Appendix 2: Orient Steam Navigation Company, 1877–1960: Fleet List of
     Passenger Ships   195

     Appendix 3: Orient Steam Navigation Company: Ships Managed by the
     Orient Line During and After World War I and World War II   207

     Bibliography   209

ACKNOWLEDGEMENTS

We would like to thank everyone who helped us create this book.

Thank you to Commodore Christopher Rynd for writing the foreword as well as his many insightful conversations about Orient Line, P&O and a life at sea.

We are thankful for the help of Janice van de Velde from the Pictures Collection of the State Library Victoria, as well as the State Library of South Australia and the National Library of Australia.

Thank you also to Suzie Cox from P&O Heritage as well as everyone who has contributed to the Henderson & Cremer collection over the years. Thanks also to Cunard Line, Ian Boyle (Simplon Postcards), Patricia Dempsey, George Frame and Christopher Rynd for providing imagery.

Finally, thanks again to our wonderful team at The History Press, particularly Amy Rigg, Alex Waite, Glad Stockdale and Martin Latham, who have supported this project from idea to reality.

Orsova 1909–36 12,036grt. A wonderful image of the days on the Australian service when ships would anchor in Port Said and gangplanks for passengers, etc. were serviced by the snaking pontoons. This view is of the *Orsova c.* 1927. (Henderson/Cremer Collection, ref. OH8533)

FOREWORD

By Commodore Christopher Rynd

From family history and old photographs of myself in a sailor suit, I know that at the age of 4 I travelled with my family from Sydney to Colombo aboard the *Orontes*, the second Orient Line vessel of that name. My early childhood was spent in the ports of Colombo and later Singapore, to which these beautiful passenger ships were frequent and prestigious callers. To me, these ships and their officers represented the pinnacle of smartness, lifestyle and professional excellence. They determined my ambition to make a career at sea as an officer in passenger liners such as these.

The history of the line was not something learnt but was naturally acquired by those who knew this era. The Orient Line ships, along with P&O ships, were the links between Britain, the 'East' and Australasia. P&O had expanded to include the British India Company in 1914 and the Orient Line in 1918, but Orient Line kept operating as a separate entity until 1960. Orient Line was one of the pioneers on the route via Suez to Australia.

As a newly qualified deck officer, my first passenger ship was the *Oronsay*, one of the post-war new-builds. She seemed

Commodore Rynd as a child on board *Orontes*. (Courtesy Commodore Rynd)

Commodore Rynd. (Courtesy of Cunard Line)

so large and grand; being part of it I felt a great sense of delight and pride. The ship that I remember most warmly is the 'old' Oriana, along with many in Australia and New Zealand and throughout the world who knew her and the beauty of her lines, innovative design, speed, sea keeping and manoeuvrability.

She was the last of an era of ships made to carry passengers, mail and high-value cargoes on line voyages from Britain via Suez to destinations east. Later in her career, she returned to Australia via North America and Panama after a summer of cruising and completing around the world voyages. When Oriana finally retired she had accrued twenty-five years of service travelling to and from Australia.

The personal history of many people, in Britain and her former colonies and now Commonwealth members, has been made on the ships of Orient Line through the places and people they met on voyages and cruises, and it now evokes many happy memories.

This book reflects the vessels that made that history.

Commodore Christopher Rynd
October 2017

Orontes II 1929–62, 19,970grt. *Orontes* preparing to test the height and clearance of the Sydney Harbour Bridge roadway on 5 November 1930. (Henderson/Cremer Collection, ref. OH6050)

INTRODUCTION

The Orient Line had a significant impact on shipping, especially in Australia and the United Kingdom. Yet today the importance of the company is relatively unknown away from maritime historians and dedicated ocean liner buffs.

Despite its undeniable impact on the development of modern Australia, the story of the Orient Line is often relegated to a chapter or two in books about P&O, largely thanks to its acquisition and eventual absorption by the larger company.

Even before they established the Orient Line, the original partners were involved in the Australian shipping trade. This was in the age of sail, when ships were often lost, timetables were difficult to maintain and financial backers were hard to come by.

This service, long forgotten in today's fast-paced world of digital communication, was a critical and essential link for the young colonies of Australia. It formed a slow but important connection between peoples of the Empire separated by tens of thousands of kilometres of unpredictable seas, and helped Australia grow from rival colonies into a nation.

In 1878 The Orient Steam Navigation Company Limited was officially formed and marked the beginning of a new era for Australia. The Orient Line was to challenge the Peninsular & Oriental Steam Navigation Company (P&O), and while they never came close to approaching the size of their larger rival, they did manage to shake up what had been up to that point a virtual monopoly on the route east of Suez and especially to Australia.

Orient Line introduced to the Australian colonies choices regarding passenger and cargo transport and their new, innovative and comfortable liners soon made them very popular for the long voyages between hemispheres.

By the late nineteenth century Orient Line had managed to win a percentage

Chimborazo 1878–1900, 3,847grt. She made twenty-four voyages on the Australian trade route before becoming a pioneering cruise ship in 1889. (Pictures Collection, State Library Victoria)

An 1880 Orient Line of Steamships poster advertising the fortnightly sailings to Australia. (Henderson/Cremer Collection, ref. OH8604)

Ormonde 1917-52, 14,852grt. Ormonde dressed overall and moored off Farm Cove in Sydney as Regatta Flagship for the Anniversary Day celebrations on 26 January 1931. (Henderson/Cremer Collection, ref. 10466)

Oronsay 1925–42, 20,001grt. February 1937
New Zealand cruise. The Orient Line was
renowned for the quality of its service.
(Henderson/Cremer Collection, ref. 11110)

of the Australian mail contract from their larger rival, forcing the two companies, Orient and P&O, to co-operate.

Even though P&O purchased a controlling share in Orient Line in 1918, for the most part Orient Line remained relatively independent for much of its history. The line's focus on long-duration voyages, coupled with an embedded culture of excellence in both ship design and customer service, saw a fleet of smart, fast liners developed, dramatically improving the conditions for their passengers.

Despite having its fleet decimated in both world wars, Orient Line endured, surviving both conflicts as well as the effects of the Great Depression.

The introduction of long-haul jet airliner services in 1958 had an impact on all of the world's shipping companies; Orient Line was no exception. Despite the unbeatable speed and efficiency of jet travel, the company pushed ahead with the construction of their final and finest ocean liner, *Oriana*.

At over 41,000 tons, *Oriana* was the largest liner to wear Orient Line colours. Her design was a significantly refined and modernised version of the Orient Line design successfully employed in her predecessors.

Fast and sleek, her interiors were modern, while her ample passenger amenities meant that she could transition to full-time cruising as the jet

airliner eclipsed passenger ships as the primary mode of global transport.

But neither *Oriana*, nor a shift to cruising, could save the Orient Line as an independently managed company, with the amalgamation of the P&O and Orient Lines in the early 1960s to create P&O-Orient. This incarnation was short-lived, with the Orient name being dropped in 1966.

But while Orient Line disappeared over fifty years ago, its legacy lives on. Not only in the naming of P&O Cruises 1995-built cruise ship *Oriana*, but in the vital work that the company did in transporting passengers and cargo to Australia and across the Empire.

A Grateful Public

The Australian colonies were very appreciative of the new Orient Line service. The Orient Line ships were of a much better standard than the ships that had previously plied the Australia to Europe routes. Most lines ran their older and less comfortable steamships on this run and it was noted in the *Evening News* on 7 September 1883 that even P&O 'did not think it necessary to send any of their best boats to this end of the Earth'.

SALVAGING HISTORY

Most of the images in this book, as well as some source material, such as board minutes and correspondence are originals.

They were saved thanks to the foresight and determination of one man who saw them as an historic resource and salvaged them from certain destruction almost fifty years ago.

In the early 1970s the P&O warehouse complex in Sydney's Darling Harbour area was being vacated for re-development. This building housed various P&O departments along with the Australian archive dating back to the 1850s, which by the 1970s also contained the important Orient Line Australian archive. It was seen as more important because the main Orient archive in London was destroyed in the bombing of London in World War II, leaving the Australian archive extant.

On hearing that a decision had been made to destroy the archive, Rob Henderson, who was then working for P&O, appealed directly to the passenger directors to save the archive and stop its destruction. His appeals to have the archive deposited with a suitable Australian Institution initially fell on deaf ears. Eventually, after lengthy discussions with Ivor Geddes, his persistence paid off and he was allowed exactly three hours one morning to save what he wanted before burning continued.

In the course of his discussions with Ivor Geddes he was told that London Head Office had no need of the archive, there was also no public body in Australia that would be suitable to take it and consequently the Board had taken the decision to burn 'the lot'.

What Rob saved in those rushed three hours forms the basis of the Henderson/Cremer Collection, which features prominently in this book.

Origins

The Orient Steam Navigation Company was formed from a desire to do what many said was impossible: operate a fleet of steamships to carry passengers and cargo to Australia around the Cape of Good Hope, without a mail contract, or some other sort of subsidy.

The first mention of the term Orient Line in Australia was in the South Australian Register of 17 October 1861 when the term 'Orient Line of Packets' was used in describing the maiden arrival of the clipper ship *Murray* in Adelaide.

The Orient Line in question referred to the London shipbroking firm Anderson, Thomson & Co. that had been running clipper ship sailings to Australia by the Cape of Good Hope since 1850.

Established in 1797 as James Thomson & Co., the firm had been joined in 1828 by 17-year-old James Anderson, who became a partner of the firm in 1842. Anderson's extended Scottish family had been involved in shipping since

the 1560s, and one of James' tasks at the firm was to manage a ship owned and captained by his uncle, Captain Alexander Anderson.

James Anderson became a driving force in the development of the company, and through his contacts James Thomson & Co. branched out, becoming a major shareholder in Thomas Bilbe's Rotherhithe shipyard in 1848.

The association of James Thomson & Co. with Australia commenced in 1850 with the ship *Charlotte Jane* and her pioneering voyage to New Zealand. The *Charlotte Jane* was one of the first four ships selected to carry the Canterbury Association colonists to New Zealand. The return voyage stopped at Sydney, collecting a full cargo including 1,699 bales of wool and 5,000 hides.

The first *Orient* was launched in 1853, and was built specifically for the Australian trade. A clipper ship, she was just over 56m long, with a beam

Though steamships were becoming common on routes around the world, the Orient Line of Clipper Ships ran to Australia with no steam power. (Frame & Cross)

The clipper ships relied on sail and had tall masts to allow them to make best use of the prevailing winds. (Frame & Cross)

of 9.66m, but before she was able to enter service she became the first ship requisitioned by the Admiralty in the Crimean War. She was used as a troopship during the war and did not begin civilian service until the middle of 1856.

In her merchant role, *Orient* was a successful ship and during her fifth round voyage to Australia the company ordered the *Murray*. Like *Orient*, *Murray* was a clipper. She was 62.48m long and sailed on her maiden voyage from London to Adelaide on 26 July 1861.

In 1863, another member of the Anderson family became a partner in the firm, and at this time the company was renamed Anderson, Thomson & Co. Six years later the last Thomson left the firm and it was once again renamed, becoming Anderson, Anderson & Co. By this time a number of other Anderson family members had joined the company.

The 1869 opening of the Suez Canal changed the face of shipping, making steamship services highly interesting for Anderson, Anderson & Co. The company was competing with a variety of other firms, including the Peninsular and Oriental Steam Navigation Company (P&O), which was already operating

Coonatto 1863–75, 633grt. An 1867 view of *Coonatto* at Port Adelaide. Typical of the famous Orient Line of Clipper Ships, the *Coonatto* was fine lined, speedy and extremely popular with passengers and shippers. (State Library of South Australia, PRG 1373/2/6)

Yatala 1865–87, 1,172grt. The *Yatala* lying centre stage in Port Adelaide in 1871. She made only seven passages from Plymouth to Adelaide, her fastest being sixty-seven days in 1867. She was lost when she went ashore off the French coast at Gris-Nez. (Pictures Collection, State Library Victoria)

Agamemnon, 1,431grt. One of the famous fully rigged Blackwall frigates, built in 1855 and owned by R. and H. Green. She served for many years on the Indian and Australian trades before being sold for use as a coal hulk in 1877. (Henderson/Cremer Collection, ref. OH9707)

Catching a Clipper

As *Orient* was preparing to sail to Adelaide, shipowner John Willis approached Captain Mitchell of the *Orient* and asked if he could take a tool chest that had been left behind by the carpenter of *Lammermuir*, and deliver the tools to him in Adelaide. Captain Mitchell refused the request, saying, 'I will take them and deliver them before I reach the line.' As *Lammermuir* had sailed from London ten days earlier, John Willis bet the captain £5 that he would not be able to achieve such a feat. However, Captain Mitchell made good as the *Orient* caught up with and hailed *Lammermuir* just north of the Equator, and the tools were rowed across for delivery to the carpenter. Both ships continued their journey to Adelaide, with *Orient* arriving six days ahead of *Lammermuir*.

steamship services to Australia via Point de Galle.

At the time of the canal opening the Orient Line of Clipper Ships was sailing to Australia via Cape Town. While steamship operators were beginning to use the Suez Canal, cutting days off the journey, the transition from the overland passage to a direct Suez transit took its toll on lines such as P&O.

Not only was P&O in need of new tonnage that could handle the longer-duration voyages, their Egyptian over-land assets such as accommodation, as well as coaling stations, had become a liability, having little value in the era of the canal.

Furthermore, a disagreement between P&O and the British Government over the carriage of the mail meant that P&O still had to transport the mail by train between Alexandria and Port Said, despite the ships making the passage via the Canal.

This presented an opportunity for other firms, including not only the Andersons but also F. Green & Co., which were operating Blackwall clipper ships to Australia and India under the banner of the Blackwall Line.

F. Green & Co. were a firm of renown, closely associated with the shipowner and shipbuilding firm of R. & H. Green. The Blackwall shipyard of R. & H. Green, located on the Thames, had been opened in 1611 and they built the ships known as the Blackwall frigates until the 1830s, at which time they began building and sailing Blackwall clippers.

Hesperus 1873–99, 1,777grt. From the Greenock yards of the famous Robert Steele, the *Hesperus* and her sister *Aurora* were magnificent in design. The *Aurora* was lost to fire after only one voyage, while the *Hesperus* became a sail training ship in both Britain and Russia. (Pictures Collection, State Library Victoria)

A fine full-sail view of the *Hesperus* in her later role as the Black Sea-based Imperial Russian Navy training ship *Grand Duchess Maria Nkolaevna*. In 1909 she was purchased by an English company and finally broken up in 1923 after an eventful fifty-year career. (Henderson/Cremer Collection, ref. OH9202)

Did You Know?

In 1875 Anderson, Anderson & Co. became chartering brokers for the fledgling Rio Tinto Co. Ltd.

Between 1869 and 1899 Anderson, Anderson and Co. was involved in the loading and operating of sailing ships, and later steamships to the West Indies. They also ran and loaded ships to North and South American ports.

While rum, sugar and pimento were common cargoes on the West Indies trade, the ships returning from Australia brought back wool, hides and minerals. Greasy and smelly, the wool was compressed into the smallest possible size, allowing more to be carried aboard the ships, and therefore bringing more profit when sold in England. However, wool was a dangerous cargo to transport by ship. When wool is compressed and wet it is also prone to spontaneous combustion and several of the Anderson, Anderson & Co. clipper ships were subject to fire as a result of their wool cargoes.

Orient was one of the ships to have a wool fire break out in 1861, though the crew were able to save her and were rewarded by the underwriters when she returned to London. *Aurora*, a later Orient Line clipper, was not so lucky as on her maiden voyage in 1875 her cargo of wool combusted and she burned down to the waterline.

The Orient clippers were, like all sailing ships, particularly at the mercy of Mother Nature, with their propulsion reliant on the winds and their size leaving them especially vulnerable to high seas. The weather during the voyage to Australia was extreme and there was the ever-present fear of icebergs at certain parts of the journey.

In addition to cargo and the usual passenger services, the Orient Line of Clipper Ships also carried British emigrants to South Australia and Queensland under contracts with their governments. Between 1876–78 the Orient Line of Clipper Ships transported 5,853 immigrants by chartered clipper ships to Queensland.

By the 1870s both Anderson and Green were exploring the prospects of steam-powered voyages. To this end, in 1872 F. Green & Co. completed an experimental steam-powered voyage to Australia with R. & H. Green's 1,255-ton steamer *Siracusa*, which sailed to Sydney.

Two years later, Anderson, Anderson & Co. partnered with F. Green & Co. for a March sailing of the steamship *Easby* to Australia. Later that year they advertised again, this time for a London to Melbourne sailing of the steamship *St Osyth*.

High Praise

Orient received praise and plaudits from both passengers and the press, even as she aged. Of her arrival at Adelaide on 24 November 1869, the *Evening Journal* commented that *Orient* looked 'as well as ever; indeed, it required no great effort of memory to recall the days of her splendour.' The article also noted that the ship was sailing so full that the captain had to take his quarters in the smoking box!

Early History of the

Orient

Steam Navigation Company

Following the success of their two steamship voyages to Australia in 1874, Anderson, Anderson and Co. decided to look further into a steamship service to Australia.

In early 1877 the shipping line approached the Pacific Steam Navigation Company (PSN Co.) and requested to charter some of their newer ships. The P.S.N. Co. had built twenty-two steamers to cater for an expected increase in their South American trade. The increase had not materialised and a number of their ships were laid up in Birkenhead. The agreement was to charter the vessels, and if the venture should prove a success there was an option to purchase.

The agreement signed 27 February 1877 was for the charter of the 3,825-ton *Lusitania* and the 3,847-ton *Chimborazo*. On 5 March 1877 they included the 3,845-ton *Cuzco* in the charter agreement.

Lusitania 1878–1900, 3,825grt. On her first voyage to Australia for the new Orient Line the *Lusitania* broke all the records, making the astounding steaming passage from Plymouth to Melbourne in forty days, six and a half hours. (Henderson/Cremer Collection, ref. OH6264)

Chimborazo 1878–1900, 3,847grt.
Chimborazo docked in Sydney for repairs to forefoot and keel after striking rocks off Point Perpendicular, near Jervis Bay, on 15 March 1878. (Henderson/Cremer Collection, ref. OH6247 Collection)

Cuzco 1878–1905, 3,845grt. Believed to be an F.C. Gould photograph of the *Cuzco*, as built, in the Thames. (Henderson/Cremer Collection, ref. OH8510)

Garonne 1878–97, 3,876grt. One of the oldest images in the collection showing the *Garonne*, as built with yards, in the Suez Canal in 1882. (Henderson/Cremer Collection, ref. OH6271)

Garonne 1878–97, 3,876grt. A later image of the *Garonne* in the River Thames, without yards. (Henderson/Cremer Collection, ref. OH6145)

Aconcagua 1878–81, 4,106grt. *Aconcagua* at the Orient Line buoy in Sydney Harbour. *Aconcagua* was the first Pacific Steam Navigation Company ship to partner in the Australian Orient Line trade. (Henderson/ Cremer Collection, ref. OH6000)

John Elder 1879–86, 3,832grt. She cuts a lonely figure gared in the Suez Canal, long before it was widened, waiting for other ships to pass in the opposite direction. *c.* 1880. (Henderson/Cremer Collection, ref. OH9301)

Orient II 1879–1910, 5,386grt. Casting shadows in the desert, *Orient*, and others in line astern in the Suez Canal, allow one of Her Majesty's troop transports to pass unheeded en route to India. (Henderson/ Cremer Collection, ref. OH8505)

Orient II 1879–1910, 5,386grt. *Orient* under way in Sydney Harbour. When built she was one of the largest steamships in the world. (Henderson/Cremer Collection, ref. 10065)

Orient II 1879–1910, 5,386grt. From the archive comes what is arguably one of the most magnificent images ever taken of the *Orient*. Most likely photographed in the Thames, the yards have been removed and she has been fitted with a turtleback. (Henderson/Cremer Collection, ref. OH6275)

Orient II 1879–1910, 5,386grt. The first-class saloon occupied the full width of the ship. This allowed natural light from portholes and from the large skylight above the open central portion of the room, which had the music room above. (Henderson/Cremer Collection, ref. P&O_261)

Orient II 1879–1910, 5,386grt. Shown in Sydney Harbour after her 1898 refit when she had two masts removed and her handsome twin funnels replaced by a single taller one. (Pictures Collection, State Library Victoria)

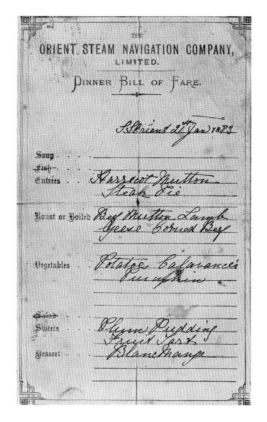

Sorata 1880–86, 4,014grt. *Sorata* and her sister *Cotopaxi* were very similar in appearance, in this image the *Sorata* is photographed in the Thames. She was very nearly lost in September 1880 when she went aground in the Backstairs Passage en route from Adelaide to Melbourne, but was successfully refloated. (Henderson/Cremer Collection, ref. OH6147)

Orient II 1879–1910, 5,386grt. A rare offering from the archive, 21 January 1883. First saloon dinner in style on board the *Orient*. Fish is off the menu but you are in for a treat with Harricot mutton, goose or the inevitable stalwart of curried beef. On this day the *Orient* was in the Arabian Sea bound for Suez. (Henderson/Cremer Collection, ref. OH10600)

Lusitania sailed from London on 26 June 1877. She called at Plymouth and left English shores carrying 345 passengers and general cargo. She arrived in Melbourne forty days later on 8 August 1877, having averaged 311 miles per day.

On her return voyage, *Lusitania* made history when she became the first steamship to sail from Australia to London via the Suez Canal.

Lusitania was followed into service by *Chimborazo* on 12 August 1877, then *Cuzco* on 25 September 1877. It was originally intended that the 3,876-ton *Garonne* would follow as the fourth

steamship in the fleet, but engine troubles delayed her entry into Orient Line service until 1878. In order to maintain their schedule, Anderson, Anderson and Co. chartered *Stad Amsterdam* from the Royal Netherlands Steamship Co. for a single round trip, departing London on 24 October 1877.

The overall venture was a success and had proved that they were capable of providing real competition for P&O.

During the course of their negotiations with P.S.N. Co., Anderson, Anderson & Co. entered discussions with F. Green & Co., who were also considering steamship services to Australia.

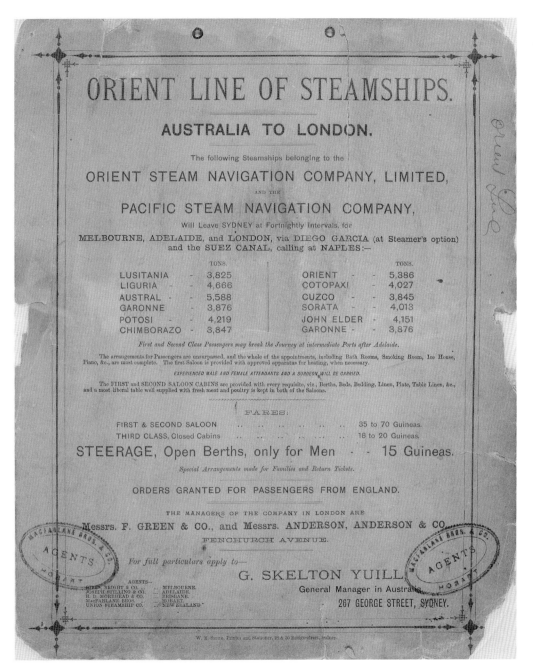

An original 1882 advertising poster for the joint service between the Orient Steam and Pacific Steam Navigation companies, Australian service. (Henderson/Cremer Collection, ref. P&O_419)

Liguria 1880–90, 4,666grt. *Liguria* with steam up and lying at anchor at the Orient Line buoy in Sydney's Neutral Bay in 1884. Having just received her coals, she is preparing to sail across to her Sydney Cove berth to embark passengers. (Henderson/Cremer Collection, ref. OH9304)

Liguria 1880–90, 4,666grt. A rare stately stern view of the *Liguria* looking splendid as she transits the Suez Canal in 1886. (Henderson/Cremer Collection, ref. OH8601)

Potosi 1880–87, 4,219grt. A superb port side view of *Potosi* in Sydney Harbour. *Potosi* made nineteen voyages to Australia in the joint service and carried 7,937 passengers. (Henderson/Cremer Collection, ref. OH9303)

Austral 1882–1903, 5,589grt. A finely detailed port side view of *Austral* in Sydney Harbour. (Henderson/Cremer Collection, ref. OH6003)

The result was that on 28 January 1878 an agreement was signed between the two, establishing their partnership.

In 1878 Anderson, Anderson & Co. and F. Green & Co. formed The Orient Steam Navigation Company Limited. The new company created a new house flag that incorporated elements of the flags of the two founding companies, Anderson, Anderson & Co. and F. Green & Co. The new company did not have a board of directors; instead the directors of Anderson, Anderson & Co. and F. Green & Co. acted as managers of the new company.

They purchased the four steamers that they had chartered from P.S.N. Co., with *Garonne* being the first

Austral 1882–1903, 5,589grt. A favourite pastime on any Australian
voyage – cricket on the first-class promenade deck on board the
Austral in 1887. (Pictures Collection, State Library Victoria)

Austral 1882–1903, 5,589grt. A sad sight, the *Austral* after she foundered whilst coaling at the Orient Line buoy in Neutral Bay on 11 November 1882. First Officer J.W. Holmes of the ship *Hallowe'en,* seen on the left, gave a graphic account of the sinking and of rousing his crew to man the boats, which rescued many of the *Austral*'s crew. (Henderson/Cremer Collection, OH6004)

vessel registered in the name of the new company.

The first sailing of the newly incorporated line left London, bound for Australia, on 17 April 1878. *Garonne* was a three-masted, single-screw vessel with a two-cylinder compound engine.

On 3 March 1878 the company purchased *Cuzco* for £78,150 and in May the *Lusitania* was bought from the P.S.N. Co. for £74,210. *Chimborazo* was the last of the four chartered liners to be purchased, in August 1878 at a cost of £72,270.

Before *Chimborazo* was acquired, during her second voyage to Australia she was damaged while sailing from Melbourne to Sydney in dense fog. On 15 March 1878 she ran onto rocks at Point Perpendicular. The forward compartment flooded but luckily the bulkhead held

and she could be refloated and taken to Jervis Bay. Once her passengers and their luggage were transferred to the steamer *Collaroy,* *Chimborazo* sailed to Sydney for repairs, arriving on 31 March under her own steam.

The dedicated Australian service was a success, and indicated to the Orient Line that it was viable to increase the frequency of their sailings. As a result the Orient Line managers decided on a monthly service and in addition to their four purchased liners they chartered the *Aconcagua* to offer the line a level of redundancy in their service. *Aconcagua* remained a P.S.N. Co. vessel, with both its officers and registration belonging to that line, though it was managed by the Orient Line.

In April 1879 the frequency of the Australian steam service was increased

Austral 1882–1903, 5,589grt. Without her yards in Sydney Harbour. (Henderson/ Cremer Collection ref. OH6006)

Austral 1882–1903, 5,589grt. In all her glory – another rare image from the collection shows the majestic *Austral* in the Suez Canal in 1882. (Henderson/Cremer Collection, ref. OH11904)

to a sailing every four weeks and this required additional tonnage. It was decided that on the Australian run the Orient liners would be supplemented by P.S.N. Co. ships. The joint service was managed and brokered by the Orient Line, with P.S.N. Co. retaining the earnings of their vessels. This meant that Orient Line were able to increase their number of sailings, though the profits of the P.S.N. Co. sailings went to P.S.N. Co. and not The Orient Steam Navigation Co.

For this purpose *John Elder* from P.S.N. Co. joined *Aconcagua*, under management by Orient Line.

Additionally, Orient Line chartered *City of London*, from City Line and *Sultan*, from R. & H. Green & Co. Both ships were used for a single round voyage to Australia with *City of London* leaving London on 30 June 1879 and *Sultan* departing on 28 July 1879.

On 5 June 1879 Orient Line celebrated a momentous occasion when their first purpose-built steamship launched at John Elder & Co., Scotland. The 5,386-ton *Orient* was a single-screw ship with a coal-fired three-cylinder compound engine. She was built with an iron hull and had two funnels and four masts. She was capable of carrying

Austral 1882–1903, 5,589grt. A delightfully whimsical view of first-class passengers in fancy dress. In the early days passengers would elect from amongst themselves an entertainments committee who would organise, with the captain's blessing, entertainments for the voyage, which always included the very popular fancy dress party. (Pictures Collection, State Library Victoria)

Iberia 1883–90, 4,671grt. *Iberia* shown in the River Thames. She made twenty Australian voyages and brought 8,043 passengers, she also made the first Orient Line call at Colombo on 10 October 1888. (Henderson/Cremer Collection, ref. OH6153)

Orizaba 1886–1905, 6,184grt. *Orizaba*, as built, in the Suez Canal. (Henderson/Cremer Collection, ref. OH6046)

3,000 tons of coal, which meant she could steam from London to Australia without re-coaling if necessary.

At her launch *Orient* was the third largest ship in the world, with only Brunel's *Great Eastern* and Inman Line's *City of Berlin* bettering her in size. She was also noted as being the first ocean steamship with a promenade deck. *Orient's* maiden voyage to Australia departed London on 1 November 1879. She arrived in Adelaide just thirty-seven days and twenty-two hours later, creating a sensation and a record.

In December Orient Line and P.S.N. Co. increased their sailings to Australia, inaugurating a joint fortnightly service. To symbolise this new agreement the Orient house flag was changed to be more similar to the P.S.N. Co. house flag.

The fortnightly service was to be run by the five ships of The Orient Steam Navigation Co., *Orient, Lusitania,* *Chimborazo, Garonne* and *Cuzco,* along with seven P.S.N. Co. ships, *Aconcagua, Iberia, John Elder, Sorata, Liguria, Cotopaxi* and *Potosi.*

The new fortnightly service was announced in *The Times of London* on 28 October 1879, in which it was stated that the expansion was justified by the increasing trade of both passengers and goods between the United Kingdom and the Australian Colonies.

P&O sent a letter of protest to P.S.N. Co. regarding the new arrangements. P&O, who had signed their first mail contract to Australia in 1852, considered that this service was their domain and that P.S.N. Co. was overstepping. P.S.N. Co. responded that their board of directors did not believe that their actions were antagonistic to the interests of P&O and reminded them that 'the connection of this Company with the direct trade to Australia has now extended over two years and that we have at present

Orizaba 1886–1905, 6,184grt. From the magnificent State Library of Victoria collection is this image of officers on the bridge of the *Orizaba* c. 1887. Moustaches in vogue and a straw boater to protect against the sun. (Pictures Collection, State Library Victoria)

Orizaba 1886–1905, 6,184grt. Another rarity, this time a Zangaki photograph of the *Orizaba*, minus yards, in the Suez Canal passing one of the Canal Company's ubiquitous dredges. (Henderson/Cremer Collection, ref. OH9306)

two steamers – the *Aconcagua* and *John Elder* – running on this Companies account in the Orient Line.'

Despite the improvements that steam technology brought to the Australian passage, it was not without peril. This was clearly demonstrated during the February 1880 sailing of *Chimborazo*. The ship left Plymouth on 8 February, but was hit by severe weather the following day. One passenger and three crew members were washed overboard and drowned, with the ship also sustaining damage. *Chimborazo* returned to Plymouth on 10 February for repairs, remaining in port for a week.

On 18 March the Australian cricket team departed Adelaide on *Garonne*, bound for England and the first test match between the two countries on English soil. The team had been formed three years earlier and had played three test matches in Melbourne prior to this journey.

By the time that *Chimborazo* left for Australia on 24 June 1880, she had been fitted with electric lighting of the incandescent type. Though the origins of the electric light can be traced back to 1802, commercially viable incandescent bulbs had only recently become available, making their appearance aboard *Chimborazo* highly innovative.

This inclusion set the vessel apart from many of her contemporaries, so much so that it attracted the attention of *The Times of London*, which, on 29 June 1880, praised the use of electric light aboard *Chimborazo*.

Initially the lighting was used modestly aboard, with selected areas such as the first-class saloon being fitted with bulbs. Additionally there was a large incandescent lantern on the open deck, which could be used when loading cargo at night.

In July 1880 *Orient* was fitted with refrigeration machinery. The technology had been tested on a number of earlier vessels but had proved its worth in February when the SS *Strathleven* had arrived in London from Sydney with a cargo of frozen meat and butter in good condition. The significance of this experimental voyage was not missed by the managers of the Orient Line. They immediately set out plans to install refrigerating machinery aboard their own vessels. They wrote to *The Times* in May 1880 that they expected that all ships in their line would carry refrigeration within a year.

Orient's first voyage with refrigeration departed in September 1880. The refrigerating machinery allowed the company to do away with the practice of carrying livestock for food and provisions. This greatly improved the atmosphere aboard the ship and freed up valuable deck space.

The most important aspect of refrigeration technology was the potential for profit. Refrigerated cargo brought good prices and broadened the range of goods that could be both imported and exported from Australia.

On 3 September the P.S.N. Co. ship *Sorata* ran aground on rocks near Cape Jervis en route from Adelaide to Melbourne on the Orient Line service. Refloating the ship took several weeks

and it was not until 15 November that this was accomplished and *Sorata* could be sent back to Adelaide for preliminary repairs. She was then sent on to Melbourne, arriving on 8 December, where she was given a more permanent fix for her badly damaged keel, returning to service in 1881.

By 1882, electric lighting had found its way to more of the Orient Line ships, including the 3-year-old *Orient*, while other ships including *Chimborazo* had seen its use widened aboard. It provided significant benefits for both passengers and crew aboard the ships, and by 1893 the whole Orient Line fleet had been fitted with some electric lighting.

As the technology became more reliable, non-passenger areas such as crew quarters, engine rooms and even the holds were illuminated by electricity, allowing the Orient Line to do away with more dangerous and dated forms of lighting such as candles and gas lamps.

On 19 May 1882 Orient Line introduced their newest liner, *Austral*, built by John Elder & Co. Glasgow. *Austral* was the second passenger steamship to be built specifically for the Orient Line's Australian service. At 138.9m long and 13.19m wide, she was longer and narrower than her forebear, *Orient*. She had many innovations, including a steam launch and a gig attached to patented davits, which allowed it to be quickly used in case of emergency. Pneumatic bells allowed passengers to contact stewards from public rooms, and there was a lift between the smoking room and the saloon bar.

Happy Passengers

After one particularly successful voyage from London to Australia in 1878, the passengers of the *Chimborazo* were so pleased that they collected contributions and presented Captain Trench with a purse containing 70 sovereigns, while Chief Officer Valler received 30 sovereigns.

Austral's maiden voyage to Australia was a success and she departed London on her second voyage on 7 September 1882. However, she was delayed en route due to a smallpox epidemic in Cape Town and again due to machinery problems, arriving in Melbourne on 30 October and Sydney on 3 November 1882. Unfortunately, *Austral*'s problems were not over.

The usual procedure for Orient Line ships arriving in Sydney was to disembark their passengers, baggage and freight alongside, if the berth was available, or by steam tender if it were not. Following this the ship would be taken to the Orient Line's buoy in Neutral Bay for coaling and cleaning. Coaling took several days and was a messy business.

On 11 November, during the coaling process *Austral* sank at the buoy as a result of a coaling error. The ship had developed a noticeable list during the coaling process. With the aft coaling ports having been left open whilst coaling in the forward ports, the ship took on water and flooded, with the tragic loss of several crew members.

Austral was not the only liner on the Australian run to suffer disaster, with the P.S.N. Co. liner *Cotopaxi* the victim of fire in December 1882 whilst loading cargo for Australia at the Royal Albert Docks in London. The damage was severe, with the interior gutted and all cargo aboard lost. *Cotopaxi* required extensive refinishing following her fire.

The refloating of the *Austral* was not a quick manoeuvre and was to be the largest engineering feat then undertaken in the Australian Colonies. It was written in *The Sydney Morning Herald* 13 March 1883 of the event:

They certainly did not anticipate that the preparatory operations would have extended over a period of fourteen or fifteen weeks, but it has been found by experience that the magnitude of the work was so great, the price at stake so valuable, the danger of making a serious mistake so apparent, and the difficulties of accomplishing such an unprecedented task in a colonial seaport so numerous, that those in authority resolved to 'hasten slowly', and, while displaying all possible expedition, to make certain of every step and guard against every imaginable contingency of failure.

The salvage of the *Austral* was a complicated undertaking, and took more than three months to complete. Work included the construction of a 125m-long cofferdam built of wood and canvas. Bulkheads were constructed within the dam to enable pumps to remove the water in a controlled manner. *Austral* was finally raised on 1 March 1883 and was towed to the head of Neutral Bay. Here she was grounded and the last of the water was removed to prepare her for repairs.

Austral sailed empty for Glasgow, via Cape Horn on 9 June 1883, for permanent repairs. The salvage operation had cost Orient Line £50,000, and in addition to the cost of repairs and the lost income from her being out of service, the company was severely impacted.

Government

Contracts

3

With both *Austral* and *Cotopaxi* out of commission for repairs, the Orient-PSN Co. service needed more tonnage in order to stick to their schedules. Adding to the difficulties was the fact that both *Lusitania* and *Orient* had been called into military service during 1882 to transport troops to Egypt as part of the British efforts to fend off the uprising led by Ahmed Ourabi. While *Orient* had been released that same year, *Lusitania* didn't return to Orient Line service until February 1883.

To bolster their fleet the Orient Line chartered the *Cephalonia* from Cunard, which completed a round voyage to Australia in early 1883. P.S.N. Co also added their ship *Iberia* to the service.

Prior to 1883, the Orient liners were not operating under a mail contract but they were still carrying mail, as recorded in the minutes of their annual general meeting on 26 April 1882:

The Company's Steamers continue to be largely used by the Imperial and Colonial Governments for the conveyance of Mails, under compulsion, and with merely nominal remuneration.

That nominal remuneration in the Australian colony of Victoria was set at 1 penny per letter and the carriage of newspapers free of charge. Nor was there any choice in the matter, with all steamers calling in Victorian ports compelled to carry mail at that rate.

There was a heavy fine for any British ship that refused to carry the mail, though the Orient Line captains did at first attempt to decline, as they were neither contracted to carry the mail nor did they have space set aside for it.

In contrast, P&O had a contract in place for carrying mail that set a price by weight for both letters and newspapers.

After lengthy negotiations, the terms for a mail contract were finally agreed between the government of the Australian colony of New South Wales (NSW) and the Orient Line. The contract commenced in September 1883, even prior to the ratification by parliament.

The rates paid to Orient Line were to be different to that paid to P&O, with letters charged at ten shillings per pound of weight and newspapers at six pennies per pound. As a result the NSW Government actually made a profit on mail, though the carriage of newspapers was at a loss.

The carriage of mail was to alternate between the Orient – P.S.N. Co. service and the P&O service, effectively making it a weekly service for the Australian colonies. The first mail was sent on the *Orient* under the terms of this contract on 21 September 1883.

Victoria did not agree to these terms, resulting in a dispute between Victoria and NSW that was not resolved for many years.

Ormuz 1886–1912 6,031grt. *Ormuz* without yards under way in Sydney Harbour with a very different nineteenth-century Sydney backdrop. (Henderson/Cremer Collection, ref. 10069)

Ormuz 1886–1912 6,031grt. A company-issued postcard of the *Ormuz* in Naples. (Henderson/Cremer Collection, ref. 10471)

ORIENT-ROYAL MAIL LINE S.S. ORMUZ
ENTERING NAPLES.

Did You Know?

The term posh comes from the acronym for port out, starboard home. On the Australian passage those who were able to secure the rooms on the port side on the voyage to Australia and starboard side on the return to England had a more comfortable journey owing to the heat of the sun.

The contract stipulated a change in the Australian service for Orient Line. With a contracted transit time of thirty-nine days, the company was obliged to have their service travel via Suez Canal both outbound and homebound.

The Suez Canal had opened in 1869; it was an event that fundamentally changed shipping routes between the United Kingdom and the Far East. The 160km waterway shaved weeks off established journey times and

Left: *Ormuz* 1886–1912 6,031grt. A finely detailed view of the *Ormuz* at an unknown port. (Henderson/Cremer Collection, ref. OH6255)

Below left: *Ormuz* 1886–1912 6,031grt. *Ormuz*, showing all the attributes of speed as she stakes her claim to the seas. (Henderson/Cremer Collection, ref. OH6269)

Above: *Oroya* 1887–1909 6,057grt. A magnificent view of the *Oroya* in the Suez Canal *c.* 1887, as built with yards on the foremast. A sister ship to *Orizaba*, *Oroya* made sixty-four Australian voyages and carried close to 20,000 passengers to Australia. (Henderson/Cremer Collection. ref. OH11905)

Above: *Oroya* 1887–1909 6,057grt. *Oroya* dressed for an unknown occasion, possibly to celebrate the Federation of Australia, a *c.* 1901 photograph. (Pictures Collection, State Library Victoria)

Above right: *Oroya* 1887–1909 6,057grt. A detailed photograph of the *Oroya* minus her yards and main mast but with heightened funnels. (Pictures Collection, State Library Victoria)

Right: *Orotava* 1890–1909 5,552grt. A magnificently detailed F.C. Gould photograph of the *Orotava* in the River Thames with the tender *Earl of Essex* alongside. (Henderson/Cremer Collection, ref. P&O_329)

resulted in long-term cost savings for shipping companies.

The Orient Line had been using the Suez route for the return journey from Australia for many years, with there being very little difference in the timings when it came to the outbound journey, owing to the favourable winds.

The transition to using the Suez Canal in both directions was not a straightforward activity. Orient Line and P&O were rivals and P&O were not keen to accommodate Orient Line at Aden where P&O had their coaling station, nor were Orient Line keen to be dependent on P&O for coal. Instead, Orient liners sailed via Diego Garcia, where the company had set up their own coaling base in 1881.

The P.S.N. Co. board were not entirely happy with the Diego Garcia enterprise

and objected to the expenditure. In June 1883 they had sent a letter to The Orient Steam Navigation Co. board stating that, 'The directors still decline to consent to the purchase of a tug for Diego Garcia and repeat that they are anxious to close the Diego Garcia account so far as this Company is concerned, even at a loss.'

The transit of the Suez Canal was complicated by how busy the waterway had become. As a result ships were often held up whilst waiting for their turn to transit the canal. With a mail service to maintain this put great pressure on the companies with those contracts. In April 1884 the Royal Mail Pennant was created. This was flown from the masts of any ships carrying the mails to or from Great Britain and allowed these ships to be easily recognised and given priority when transiting busy waterways and ports, including the Suez Canal, .

On 15 August 1884, Orient Line and the South Australian Government came to an agreement on the carriage of mail to Adelaide. The agreement outlined a penalty of £300 per voyage if, for any reason other than complete breakdown, the Orient Line ships did not call at Adelaide on their voyage. The terms of payment were 12s per pound weight of letters, 1s per pound weight of packets and 6d per pound weight of newspapers.

In addition to the mail contract with the Government of New South Wales, it was also agreed that Orient Line would transport assisted immigrants to the growing colony. Orient Line was paid £15 per person up to 400 people, with a slightly reduced tariff of £14 10d for the next 200 people.

Between December 1883 and January 1887, Orient Line chartered a number of vessels from various lines to run their

Above left: *Orotava* 1890–1909 5,552grt. Port side view of *Orotava* under way in Sydney Harbour. (Henderson/Cremer Collection)

Above right: *Oruba* 1890–1905 5,552grt. *Oruba* as built lying alongside at Barrow-in-Furness. (Henderson/Cremer Collection, ref. OH6256)

Canal Crisis

The opening of the Suez Canal was a significant achievement. Nonetheless, for many years there were considerable delays to ships transiting the waterway because of its design. In some locations the width of the canal was only 22.86m, which meant that ships could not pass each other. To deal with this issue the narrow parts of the canal maintained one-way traffic during certain times of the day. Ships travelling in the opposite direction were required to moor until the direction of traffic was reversed. To allow ships travelling in the opposite direction to pass, one lane was required to tie up until the canal was cleared. There were twenty-four points at which this occurred.

emigrant services. The chartered ships included Great Western Steamship Co.'s *Warwick Castle*, Anchor Line's *Belgravia*, Cunard Line's *Parthia* and Aberdeen Line's *Aberdeen*. In all they made twenty-six contracted voyages and carried more than 16,000 emigrants from Britain to Sydney.

In 1885 *Lusitania* was once again chartered for Admiralty service, this time as an armed merchant cruiser. She remained under charter for six months due to the Russian invasion of Afghanistan and the heightened tensions between the British Empire and the Russian Empire.

In February 1886, having been returned to her owners, *Lusitania* was sent to J. Richardson and Sons for refit. During the refit *Lusitania* was fitted with new boilers and engines of the triple-expansion type.

In September that year Orient Line had cause to celebrate when their new ship, *Ormuz,* was launched at the Fairfield Shipbuilding & Engineering Company in Glasgow. *Ormuz* was the third ship built specifically for The Orient Steam Navigation Co.; she was built with a double bottom and was their biggest ship yet. She was fitted with triple-expansion engines and was designed to complete the England to Australia journey in twenty-eight sailing days.

Ormuz used hydraulics to operate the winches and windlasses, rather than the traditional method of using steam power. This was a great improvement, as it meant that it was no longer necessary to run steam pipes around passenger cabins, and thus reduced an overheating problem. Additionally, she had mechanical ventilation as well as stale air extraction in every compartment aboard.

Affectionately known as the greyhound, *Ormuz* departed London on her maiden voyage on 3 February 1887 and arrived in Adelaide on 11 March. She was received with much enthusiasm by the Australian public and quickly settled in to her role.

P.S.N. Co.'s new ship, *Oroya*, also commenced sailing for the Australian service in February 1887 and there was some friendly rivalry regarding which of the two new ships was the fastest.

In 1887 Orient Line was finally able to put the *Austral* sinking behind them after their litigation against the Ocean Marine Insurance Company was settled in their favour. The original claim, for costs relating to the raising of the *Austral*, had been only paid at 55 per cent of the total claim. Orient Line had disputed this and the insurance company was ordered to pay the additional amount, including costs.

In August 1887 it was decided to re-engine *Cuzco* and she was taken out of service, not returning until early 1888. Like *Lusitania*, *Cuzco* was given new boilers and triple-expansion engines. In addition she was given an extensive internal refurbishment to bring her up to current standards. The yards and topgallants were also removed from her foremast and main mast.

In January 1888 a mail contract was agreed with the British Government. Orient Line and P&O each bid for a

PLEASURE CRUISES.

THE ORIENT COMPANY *despatch, from time to time, some of their* Steamers on SPECIAL YACHTING CRUISES, *occupying periods ranging from 2 to 8 weeks,*

To NORWAY,

(LAND OF THE MIDNIGHT SUN),

VISITING   ROMSDAL.

THE FINEST FIORDS,

AND CALLING AT

BERGEN, TRONDHJEM, HAMMERFEST, LOFOTEN ISLANDS, NORTH CAPE, &C.

BERGEN.

TO THE MEDITERRANEAN, LEVANT, & BLACK SEA, VISITING

ALGIERS, ATHENS, PALERMO. NAPLES, THE RIVIERA, MALTA, SMYRNA, CONSTANTINOPLE, SEBASTOPOL, BALACLAVA, YALTA, &c.,

ALSO TO   ROME.

PALESTINE & EGYPT.

And to MADEIRA, CANARY ISLANDS, and other places of Interest,

ACCORDING TO THE SEASON.

ATHENS.

An early 1890s Orient Line 'Yachting Cruise' advertisement. The Orient Line pioneered deep-sea cruising in 1889 with their steamer *Chimborazo,* which helped to lay the foundations for today's cruise ship industry. (Henderson/Cremer Collection, ref. OH11906)

Did You Know?

In 1882 the *Sorata* was compelled to carry the mail from Australia to London. Captain Dixon promised to take care of it but made it clear that the ship had no room set aside for the mail and he would have to carry it on deck, under a tarpaulin and could not be responsible for its condition on arrival.

share of the contract and were both successful, with the new arrangement delivering the first weekly mail service to Australia under British contract. The schedule was delivered by the Lines, which called in Australia on alternate weeks.

Adelaide remained the Australian port at which the mail was disembarked and loaded onto fast trains for onward delivery. In Europe, Orient Line used the port of Naples, while P&O operated via Brindisi, Italy for the fast dispatch of the mail trains across continental Europe for delivery to London.

The new contract came into effect on 1 February 1888 and specified that the Orient Line would make the journey between Adelaide and Naples in thirty-two days, and P&O in thirty-two and a half days. This contract also solidified Colombo as a permanent port of call for ships travelling in both directions, with Diego Garcia dropped in favour of Aden for coaling.

The new mail contract stipulated that the Orient Line ships call at Colombo on both their eastbound and westbound journeys. A benefit of this revised itinerary was that the vessels could collect cargo for their onward journey. *Iberia,* which had entered the Australian service with the stipulation that she would not call at Diego Garcia, inaugurated the Orient Line calls to Colombo.

To service the new contract, in 1889 Orient Line ordered a new ship from Robert Napier and Sons in Glasgow. To be named *Ophir,* the new ship was to be a vessel of approximately 7,000 tons and the largest of the fleet built so far.

In 1889 Orient Line also began to offer pleasure cruises in the Australian off-season. On 12 March *Chimborazo* embarked on a thirty-seven-day cruise to the Mediterranean. The ship departed London and called at Lisbon, Gibraltar, Algiers, Palermo, Naples, Livorno, Genoa, Nice, Malaga and Cadiz before returning to London. The brochure advertised *Chimborazo* as a modern ship, fitted with 'electric light, hot and cold baths, etc. Cuisine of the highest order'.

The cruise was a success and *Chimborazo* and *Garonne* were withdrawn from the Australian service in May and June of 1889. After brief refits they started the world's first regular cruising schedule from London.

Into the Future

4

In 1890 the last of the Orient Line clipper ships were sold. Although never held under The Orient Steam Navigation Company, the clipper ships owned by Anderson, Anderson & Co. had continued to offer cargo and passenger services to Australia under the name of the Orient Line of Clipper Ships. Crew lists show that officers and captains would transfer between the clipper ships and steamships, even though they were operated as separate entities.

The last clipper ship built for the Andersons' Australian service had been *Harbinger* and both she and the slightly older *Hesperus* made sailings in the final months of the clipper service. *Hesperus* was the last to return to port in May 1890 and both ships were later sold to Devitt and Moore for further use.

The great property crash of 1891 in Australia was to cause difficulties for the Orient service. Land values had fallen by almost 50 per cent, with several banks failing. The downturn lasted roughly five years and impacted on the profitability of all lines trading with Australia.

On 30 October 1891 *Ophir* was delivered by Robert Napier and Sons. *Ophir* was the first twin-screw ship built for the Australian service. She had two funnels and two unrigged masts. As with many merchant ships built at the time, she was built with the potential to be converted to an armed merchant cruiser. In aid of this potential purpose, *Ophir*'s boiler rooms were spaced apart, with the idea that this would offer protection in the event of the ship coming under fire.

Unfortunately *Ophir* was a very expensive ship to run. Her coal consumption was very high, using over 120 tons per day. Various methods were tried to reduce her coal usage, running her slow, fast and in cruising mode, but nothing worked.

The build of *Ophir* had not been as smooth as Orient Line might have hoped, with the shipyard and company having a dispute that ended in arbitration. In 1892, £35,420 was repaid to Orient Line over the dispute.

Also in 1892 the Victorian Government introduced the Life-Saving Appliances amendment to the Marine Act 1890. The new regulations required ships to carry lifeboats 'placed under davits, fit and ready for use, and having proper appliances for getting them into the water' with the number and capacity outlined in a table that related size of the vessel to number of boats.

The new regulations were designed to ensure lifeboat space for every person on board in event of an emergency. The new regulations also specified the quantity and location of other life-saving equipment including life belts, life buoys and inextinguishable lights. As a result of these new regulations, Orient Line spent £3,379 on carrying out improvements and repairs to their vessels.

Ophir 1891–1918 6,910grt. A rare view of the magnificent *Ophir*, Orient Line's first twin-screw steamer, the largest and the most opulent to trade East of Suez, and also the most expensive to operate. (Henderson/Cremer Collection, ref. 10022)

Ophir 1891–1918 6,910grt. Seen here as H.M.Y. *Ophir*. Fitted out and painted white with a gold-edged royal blue band around the hull, the *Ophir* looked every inch a Royal Yacht. (Henderson/Cremer Collection, ref. P&O_330)

Ophir 1891–1918 6,910grt. A wonderfully detailed portside view of the *Ophir* lying quietly in Sydney Harbour. (Henderson/Cremer Collection, ref. OH9401)

Ophir 1891–1918 6,910grt. A rare view of H.M.Y. *Ophir* alongside at Hobart. As a Royal Yacht the *Ophir* carried the Duke and Duchess of Cornwall and York on a tour of the Empire in 1901. (Henderson/Cremer Collection, ref. OH6182)

Ophir 1891–1918 6,910grt. The Duke and Duchess of Cornwall and York, Prince George and Princess Mary, later to become King George V and Queen Mary, were the principal passengers on the Imperial cruise of the *Ophir* in 1901. In this photograph they are accompanied by Princess Mary's brother, Prince Alexander of Teck. He relinquished his German titles during World War I and became Earl of Athlone and later Governor-General of Canada. (Henderson/Cremer Collection, ref. P&O_256)

Did You Know?

The 'Federation Drought' – a series of dry spells in Australia around the time of federation – caused a strain on Orient Line's cargo services.

Ophir 1891–1918 6,910grt. As the Royal Yacht, Ophir was fitted out for Royal travel. The state dining room was the full width of the ship, surmounted by a large arched dome decorated with painted glass. Carved female figures stood on niches holding gold-plated chains that supported the electric lights. Carved into the arched walls of the dome were the Imperial and Australian colonial coats of arms and figures of industry. (Henderson/Cremer Collection, OH)

From February 1892 to April 1893 Lusitania was chartered by P.S.N. Co. for use on their South American service.

Once back in Orient Line service Lusitania remained on the Australian run, although she joined Garonne in a cruising role during the off-season. Other ships of the line, including Orient and Ophir, also undertook cruising itineraries.

On 9 October 1894 Chimborazo was sold to P.J. Pitcher of Liverpool, to continue as a cruise ship by the name of Cleopatra. Garonne left the fleet three years later, sold to John Porter of Liverpool for over £9,000. Porter then sold her to F. Waterhouse in the United States, where she operated in a trooping capacity during the Spanish–America war. She was eventually scrapped in 1905.

In 1897 a new mail contract was entered into with the British Government. The contract was again awarded to Orient Line and P&O jointly and required the service to be undertaken

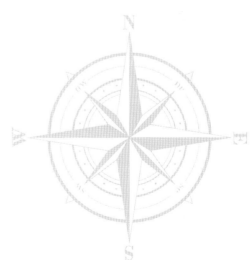

Above: *Ophir* 1891–1918 6,910grt. A splendid view of the Royal Yacht *Ophir* at Portsmouth. (Henderson/Cremer Collection, ref. P&O_169)

Above right: *Ophir* 1891–1918 6,910grt. An interesting photograph of *Ophir* equipped with a Suez Canal searchlight, over the bow, indicating that she is about to or has made a night passage of the canal. (Henderson/Cremer Collection, ref. P&O_331)

Right: *Omrah* 1899–1918 8,291grt. A lovely image of *Omrah* in Sydney Harbour. (Henderson/Cremer Collection, ref. 10007)

Omrah 1899–1918 8,291grt. First-class two-berth cabin on the *Omrah*, fitted out for comfort turn-of-the-century style. (Henderson/Cremer Collection, ref. OH6263)

Omrah 1899–1918 8,291grt. A wonderful stern starboard view of *Omrah* making a turn in Sydney Harbour off Neutral Bay. (Henderson/Cremer Collection, ref. OH9402)

Omrah 1899–1918 8,291grt. A wonderful view of the second-class saloon on *Omrah*. Note the swivel chairs anchored to the deck. The seats were reversible for either hot or cool climate comfort. (Henderson/Cremer Collection, ref. OH6270)

ORIENT LINE S.S. OMRAH.
Twin Screw 8791 Tons reg 10,000 Horse Power
SECOND SALOON.

in twenty-nine days between Naples and Adelaide for Orient Line and twenty-eight and a half days between Brindisi and Adelaide for P&O. The new contract came into effect in 1898.

In late 1897 the decision was made to re-engine the ageing *Orient*. She was sent to Wallsend Slipway Company in December of that year, where she remained for more than six months. She was given triple-expansion engines and her masts and funnels were replaced with two unrigged masts and a single large funnel. Her passenger accommodation also underwent a significant refurbishment, and forecastle and turtle decks were constructed. All in all it

was a very different-looking *Orient* that returned to service in June 1898. Her new appearance received mixed reviews.

At the Fairfield Shipbuilding and Engineering Company yard in Glasgow, the latest Orient Liner was taking shape and on 3 September 1898 it was time for the launch. Unfortunately it wasn't until the next day that she left the slipway, as she drifted back onto it following the initial launch. Tugs were required to move her off the slipway and into the fitting out basin.

The new ship was named *Omrah* and was handed over to Orient Line on 30 January 1899. She was a twin-screw ship with triple-expansion engines,

Omrah 1899–1918 8,291grt. An undated photograph of *Omrah* passing Sydney Cove on one of her fifity-five departures from Sydney. (Henderson/Cremer Collection, ref. 10070)

Did You Know?

After being a Royal Yacht *Ophir* was nicknamed 'Queen of the Indian Ocean'.

Omrah 1899–1918 8,291grt. An unusual view of *Omrah* showing her slim lines and very tall funnel. (Henderson/Cremer Collection, ref. OH11911)

and had a single large funnel that was more than 70ft high. There was accommodation for 850 passengers, of whom 500 were carried in third class and the rest in first and second. *Omrah* departed on her maiden voyage to Australia on 3 February.

The Express and Telegraph (Adelaide) called *Omrah* 'undoubtedly the finest boat all round engaged in Antipodean trade'. *Omrah* was more economical to run than the *Ophir*, and also more comfortable for passengers. As a result she quickly became more popular than her older fleet mate.

With the start of the Second Boer War in 1899, *Orient* was called into government service as troop ship number 24

Right: *Ortona* 1899–1906 7,945grt. A close-up postcard view of the *Ortona*. Her Australian service was interrupted in 1902 when she was requisitioned for service as a troop transport during the Boer War. (Henderson/Cremer Collection, ref. 10669)

Below left: *Ortona* 1899–1906 7,945grt. A company-issued postcard view of the *Ortona*. (Henderson/Cremer Collection, P&O_194.077)

Below right: *Orontes* 1902–1922 9,023grt. A larger version of the *Omrah*, the *Orontes* made fifty-four mail voyages on the Australian service and carried 23,594 passengers. (Henderson/Cremer Collection, ref. 10002)

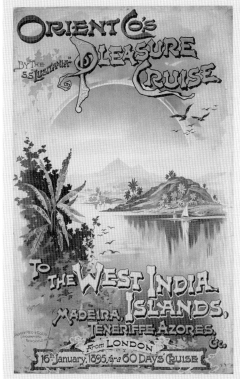

Orontes 1902–22 9,023grt. A company postcard showing the Orontes. (Henderson/Cremer Collection, ref. 10494)

and was the first steamer to transport frozen meat to the troops in southern Africa. She remained in government service for more than three years.

In August 1899 Lusitania suffered damage when she collided with a break-water in Copenhagen. She had been cruising full time since her withdrawal from the Australian service in early 1898. In February 1900 Lusitania was sold, and in 1901 she ran aground north of Cape Race and was a total loss.

The Second Boer War saw another Orient Line vessel chartered by the Admiralty when Austral spent two months from February 1900 operating as a troop carrier.

Ormuz became the first Orient Line steamship to call at the newly developed port of Fremantle, Western Australia, when she visited on 13 August 1900. This marked the beginning of regular calls to the port as Fremantle became the first and last Australian port of call for the England–Australia–England mail steamers.

In August 1900 the original company, The Orient Steam Navigation Company Limited was wound up and a new company, Orient Steam Navigation Company Limited ('The' was removed from the name) was begun. The existing shareholders were offered a choice between taking up like-for-like value of deferred shares or preferred shares at a value of 60 per cent of their current holdings. Those who did not choose either option could have their shares

Lusitania 1878–1900 3,825grt. A beautifully descriptive poster advertising a sixty-day cruise in 1896 by the Lusitania from London to the West Indies. It was yet another indication that the Orient Line considered cruising as a major development in their future. (P&O Heritage)

Orontes 1902–22 9,023grt. An old and damaged photograph from the Orient Line Archive but one which shows the fine-looking proportions of *Orontes*. (Henderson/Cremer Collection, ref. 10009)

Orontes 1902–22 9,023grt. A very early postcard showing *Orontes* alongside the Orient Line wharf, which was then on the eastern side of Sydney's Circular Quay. (Henderson/Cremer Collection, ref. 10497)

At times gold, to the value of millions of pounds sterling, would be on the high seas in Orient Line ships en route from Australia to London. Before the port of Fremantle was built ships always called at Albany in King George's Sound, the last Australian port-of-call, and would take on board the best that the goldfields of Kalgoorlie could produce. This 1897 photograph shows boxes of gold about to be taken down and loaded on the waiting Orient liner. (Henderson/Cremer Collection, ref. OH10606)

bought back at 60 per cent of their face value.

Re-establishing the company allowed Orient Steam Navigation Co. to adjust the existing capital and reallocate the balance to the depreciation account, thus reducing the value of their fleet on the books. This in turn made the company more profitable, by more closely aligning the actual value of their ships with their paper value.

In December 1900 *Ormuz* collided with the cargo vessel *Ismaila* while the latter ship was entering the port of Melbourne. Both ships suffered damage to their bows, but were able to make port under their own power. Once in port, *Ormuz*'s passengers and cargo were disembarked and she was sent for repairs. The repairs took more than eight weeks to complete and *Ormuz* did not resume her journey home until February 1901.

That same December *Ophir* was chartered by the Admiralty for use as the Royal Yacht for the Duke and Duchess of Cornwall and York's, later King George V and Queen Mary, 1901 tour of the Empire. Under the supervision of the Admiralty Transport Department, refurbishment work was undertaken by the Orient Line. The work was substantial; various rooms were converted to suit the purposes of the royal household, yards were installed

Did You Know?

An old Orient Line legend has it that whenever the *Ophir* set sail, management would groan at the thought of what the voyage would cost them!

Orontes 1902-22 9,023grt. A programme for a farewell concert given on board the RMS *Orontes*, on the spar deck 27 February 1906, in the Indian Ocean. (Henderson/Cremer Collection, ref. folio 1-100025)

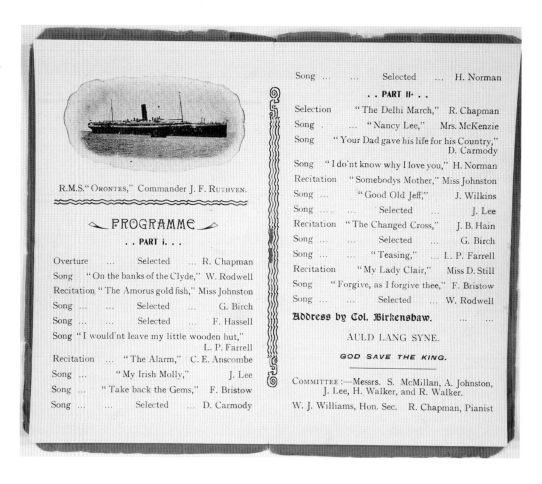

R.M.S. "ORONTES," Commander J. F. RUTHVEN.

PROGRAMME

.. PART i. ..

Overture	... Selected	... R. Chapman
Song	"On the banks of the Clyde,"	W. Rodwell
Recitation	"The Amorus gold fish,"	Miss Johnston
Song	... Selected	... G. Birch
Song	... Selected	... F. Hassell
Song	"I would'nt leave my little wooden hut,"	L. P. Farrell
Recitation	... "The Alarm,"	C. E. Anscombe
Song	"My Irish Molly,"	J. Lee
Song	"Take back the Gems,"	F. Bristow
Song	... Selected	... D. Carmody
Song	... Selected	... H. Norman

. . PART II· . .

Selection	"The Delhi March,"	R. Chapman
Song	"Nancy Lee,"	Mrs. McKenzie
Song	"Your Dad gave his life for his Country,"	D. Carmody
Song	"I do'nt know why I love you,"	H. Norman
Recitation	"Somebodys Mother,"	Miss Johnston
Song	"Good Old Jeff,"	J. Wilkins
Song	... Selected	... J. Lee
Recitation	"The Changed Cross,"	J. B. Hain
Song	... Selected	... G. Birch
Song	"Teasing,"	... L. P. Farrell
Recitation	"My Lady Clair,"	Miss D. Still
Song	"Forgive, as I forgive thee,"	F. Bristow
Song	... Selected	... W. Rodwell

Address by Col. Birkensbaw. ... ...

AULD LANG SYNE.

GOD SAVE THE KING.

COMMITTEE :—Messrs. S. McMillan, A. Johnston, J. Lee, H. Walker, and R. Walker.

W. J. Williams, Hon. Sec.   R. Chapman, Pianist

Did You Know?

In 1901 *Ormuz* transported royal carriages to Australia that were to be used by the Duke and Duchess of Cornwall and York during their royal tour.

on her masts to comply with Admiralty signalling requirements and special royal barges were fitted.

The Duke and Duchess visited the ship in February to inspect the works and on 15 March they embarked for their eight-month round voyage. King Edward VII and Queen Alexandra visited the ship the following day, just prior to *Ophir*'s departure.

On the royal tour *Ophir* called at Gibraltar, Malta, Port Said, Suez, Aden, Colombo, Singapore, Albany, Melbourne, Sydney, Auckland, Wellington, Littleton, Hobart, Adelaide, Albany, Fremantle, Mauritius, Durban, Simonstown, St Vincent, Quebec, Halifax and St John's.

The call in Melbourne coincided with the opening of the first Australian Commonwealth Parliament on 9 May 1901. Australia had united in federation on 1 January 1901 with the first elections for parliament occurring in March of that year. The first parliament was in the Exhibition Building in Melbourne and the Duke of Cornwall and York officially opened parliament in front of 12,000 guests.

Ophir arrived back in Plymouth on 31 October 1901. The following day the ship made its way to the Solent, for final docking in Portsmouth. King Edward VII and Queen Alexandra again visited the ship before they all departed. With the royal party disembarked the ship returned to the Orient Line and was refurbished for passenger service, returning to the trade on 3 January 1902. Though she was still uneconomical to run, her royal engagement had made her extremely popular.

From 1901 Orient Line started marketing its Australian sailings under the Orient Pacific Line brand. This was an attempt to both strengthen the partnership between Orient and P.S.N. Co. and also enable stronger competition with P&O.

In 1902 Orient Line launched a new ship at Fairfield Shipbuilding and Engineering Company. *Orontes* was launched on 10 May and handed over to Orient Line on 12 September that same year.

Orontes was 9,023 tons and the first Orient Line vessel to be fitted with quadruple expansion engines. She had a single funnel and two masts, and could achieve 18 knots. Her interiors were modern and British, with no excessive ornateness. She departed from London on her first Australian voyage on 24 October 1902.

In May 1903 *Austral* left the fleet. She had been sold to an Italian ship breaker for £13,250, which was more

than the price she stood at in the Orient Line accounts.

Less than two years later, Orient Line sold yet another of their ships for scrap. The *Cuzco* was by now 34 years old and had ceased sailings to Australia in 1902. She had been used as a cruise ship in her final years. *Cuzco* was the last of the original four steamers purchased from P.S.N. Co. and with her retirement the Orient Steam Navigation Co. fleet now numbered five vessels: *Orient*, *Ormuz*, *Ophir*, *Omrah* and *Orontes*.

A 1903 Orient Line forty-page cruise brochure announcing a cruise by the *Cuzco* to ports in the Baltic Sea. A noticeable feature of the cruise was the time in ports – two days twenty-one hours in Copenhagen, three days in Stockholm and seven days thirteen hours in St Petersburg – which allowed ample time for an excursion to Moscow or Nizhny Novgorod. (Henderson/Cremer Collection, ref. OH11800)

5

The Break Up

Orient Line's contract for the Australian mail service, which had been negotiated with the British Government, terminated on 31 January 1905. The new mail contract was negotiated with the Australian Government and was to run for three years. Though Orient Line once again won a portion of the contract, there were difficulties to overcome.

On 17 February 1905 the P.S.N. Co. ship *Orizaba*, operating on the Orient Line service, ran aground off Rottnest Island on the approach to Fremantle. She had been sailing from Colombo and had been enveloped in a thick haze caused by bushfires burning along the coast of Western Australia. *Orizaba* had failed to see the light on Rottnest Island and had struck Five Fathom Bank in the early morning. She was a total loss.

The Australian Government ratified the new mail agreement in 1906 and very soon after gave notice that they intended to terminate the contract at its completion. There was a feeling from the Australian public that the Orient Line and P&O services were unnecessarily expensive and that the British shipping companies were in collusion to drive up the cost of freight to the detriment of Australian merchants.

This feeling had been exacerbated by the 1904 Australian Royal Commission into the butter industry. One of the aspects that had been under

Orsova 1909–36 12,036grt. The first of the 12,000-ton liners, built from 1909, to modernise the Orient Line fleet, *Orsova* made a remarkable seventy-three Australian mail voyages and carried 47,575 passengers. (Henderson/Cremer Collection, ref. 10793)

Orsova 1909–36 12,036grt. An impressive view of *Orsova* in Port Philip Bay. She was the leading ship of her class, which brought the Orient Line into a new era of independence on the England and Australia Royal Mail service. (Pictures Collection, State Library Victoria)

R.M.S. ORSOVA.

Orsova 1909–36 12,036grt. A great starboard view of *Orsova* showing the developing Orient Line style with the bridge further aft, a feature first noticed with the *Omrah* ten years earlier. (Henderson/Cremer Collection, ref. OH6055)

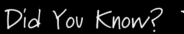

Did You Know?

The Orient Line House Flag was once again changed in 1908, this time to differentiate their service from P.S.N. Co. and Royal Mail Steam Packet Company.

Orsova 1909–36 12,036grt. A company-issued view of a cabine de luxe, showing the sitting room with the bathroom beyond. This was in the days before air conditioning, so the cabin has been provided with a fan and ceiling hooks to hold open the porthole for that extra breeze when required. (Henderson/Cremer Collection, ref. OH6258)

A wonderful 1910 Orient Line poster from the pen of Giovanni Barbaro. It captured all the exoticism and romance of the Suez Canal route to and from Australia and the East. (PO Heritage)

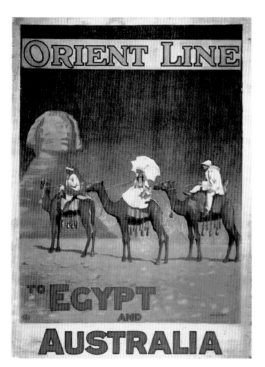

investigation was the freight cost of butter, which was mostly being carried by the mail steamers to Britain. The question had been raised as to why the freight cost for butter was so high, being £7 per ton, when the price of freight for other refrigerated items, such as rabbits, was considerably lower. As a result, Australian butter manufacturers were severely disadvantaged by the inconsistent and unfair pricing for freight.

The results of the 'butter commission' were widely publicised in the newspapers and with other more competitively priced shipping lines, for example Norddeutscher Lloyd, offering services to Australia, it was felt that neither Orient Line nor P&O deserved to win the new contract.

The Mail Services Commission took tenders from both companies, but dismissed their submissions that their fees were the lowest amount reasonable for completing the service. Instead, the new contract was awarded to Sir James Laing & Sons, were was going to build a new line of steamers to cater to the Australian trade. The new mail steamers were to be modern, fast and in every way superior to the ships currently running the Australian mail contract.

The Orient Line responded to the news, and at the Orient annual general meeting on 24 April 1907. The chairman, Frederick Green, stated:

Otway 1909–17 12,077grt. An excellent view of the *Otway* in Sydney Harbour in 1910. Although from different builders, the *Otway* was a sister ship to both *Orsova* and *Osterley*. (Henderson/Cremer Collection, ref. 10004)

Otway 1909–17 12,077grt. Once the preserve of first-class passengers only, the boat deck was the principal area for sports and games, played around the ephemera of the ship such as lifeboats and the inevitable pre-air conditioning air scoops, which could be turned to capture every breeze and sent down to ventilate the lower decks and the engine rooms. (Henderson/Cremer Collection, ref. 10587)

Did You Know?

In March 1909 *Orontes* carried the Australian cricket team to England to defend the Ashes.

Otway 1909–17 12,077grt. Under tow, steaming and looking good in Port Philip Bay on her way to her berth. (Pictures Collection, State Library Victoria)

Otway 1909–17 12,077grt. A wonderfully atmospheric illuminated view of *Otway* alongside in Hobart in 1912, loading apples for the London markets. (Henderson/ Cremer Collection, ref. 10039)

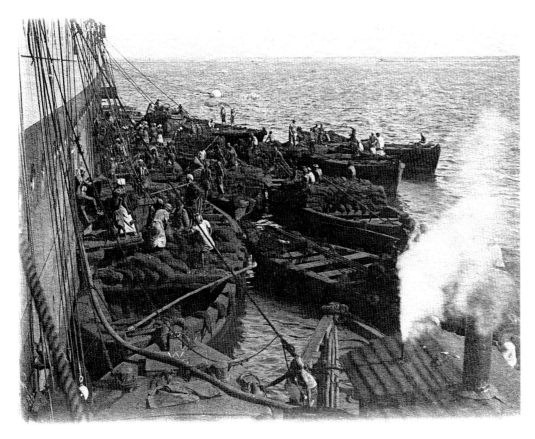

Until the early 1920s all Orient Line ships were driven by coal-fired engines, which meant that the ship's coal bunkers had to be frequently replenished during the voyage. It was hot, dusty and dirty work. In this image sacks of coal are hauled up and emptied down the coal shutes to the bunkers alongside the engine rooms. (Henderson/Cremer Collection, ref. OH5902)

Osterley 1909–30 12,129grt. RMS. *Osterley* looking trim and making speed as she departs Sydney in March 1913. (Henderson/ Cremer Collection, ref. 10794)

Osterley 1909–30 12,129grt. The third ship of the Orsova Class, *Osterley* made fifty-seven Australian mail voyages and brought 43,107 passengers to Australia. (Henderson/Cremer Collection, ref. OH6056)

Otranto 1909–18 12,124grt. *Otranto*'s beautifully designed first saloon music room, elegantly furnished by Waring & Gillow of London and surmounted by an ornate stained-glass dome. (Henderson/Cremer Collection, ref. 11308)

Opposite: *Osterley* 1909–30 12,129grt. *Osterley*'s 'black gang', the men who kept the furnaces fed with coal and worked in oppressive and dangerous conditions. (Henderson/Cremer Collection, ref. OH9404)

Otranto 1909-1918 12,124grt. A superb port side view of *Otranto* in Sydney Harbour. (Henderson/Cremer Collection, ref. 10003)

Otranto 1909–18 12,124grt. A splendid image of *Otranto* making an early morning arrival at Melbourne. (Pictures Collection, State Library Victoria)

Orvieto 1909–31 12,130grt. A classic view of *Orvieto* undergoing her speed trials on the Clyde. (Henderson/Cremer Collection, ref. 10556)

R.M.S. ORVIETO.

Orvieto 1909–31 12,130grt. A
company-issued postcard view of the
Orvieto. (Henderson/Cremer Collection,
ref. 10557)

R.M.S. "ORVIETO."

(By kind permission of Capt. Ruthven.)

✳ **Programme of Concert** ✳

HELD ON

Thursday, December 16, 1909.

Chair to be taken by E. P. KOE Esq. at 9 o'clock.

Pianoforte Selection	...	...	Mrs. Gluckstein
Song	...	"The Rosary"	Miss Devlin
Song	...	"Don't cry, little girl"	Mr. E. P. Koe
Song	...	"Awake"	Miss Blackett
Song	...	"Glorious Devon"	Mr. A. Newman
Song	...	"Philosophy"	Miss Read
Song	...	Selected	Dr. Stanley Noble
Pianoforte Selection	...	...	Mr. F. E. Parsons
Recitation	...	Selected	Miss N. Veitch
Song	"Eyes that used to gaze in mine"		Miss Devlin
Song	...	"I had a flower"	Mr. A. Newman
Song	...	"The Old Home"	Miss Blackett
Song	...	"Three for Jack"	Mr. R. S. Hicks
Song	...	"My dear soul"	Miss Read

GOD SAVE THE KING.

Orvieto 1909–31 12,130grt. Programme
for a first saloon concert held on board
during Orvieto's maiden 1909 voyage
to Australia. The concert was organised
by the passengers' entertainment
committee, which was elected at the
start of the voyage and organised
all the entertainments during the
voyage. (Henderson/Cremer Collection,
ref. folio 1_00060)

If the new contractors can do what they have undertaken, and show a profit, we shall have to confess to a grave miscalculation.

In addition to being advised that they were to lose the mail contract, Orient Line was also facing dissension within their operating partnership. P.S.N. Co. had given notice that they wished to terminate their agreement with Orient Line at the end of their current contract and so Orient Steam Navigation Co. were required to find a new running partner.

Their new partner was Royal Mail Steam Packet Company. To complete the service, Royal Mail purchased the P.S.N. Co. steamers that were already running on the Australian route, *Oruba, Oroya, Ortona* and *Orotava*. The new service was marketed under Orient Royal Mail and the Orient liners adopted the buff-coloured funnels of the Royal Mail Line to unify the fleets. But the new relationship was to be an uneasy one, with the larger Royal Mail taking a somewhat heavy-handed approach towards their new partners.

In May 1906 *Ormuz* was involved in an incident whilst transiting the Suez Canal. She was attempting to overtake the Anchor Line's *Assyria* but came too close, causing *Assyria*, in an attempt to avoid collision, to run aground. The Admiralty Court held *Ormuz* to blame for the incident.

Above: *Orama* 1911–17 12,927grt. Decorated in Louis XVI style, the elegant first-class lounge with the main staircase in the centre beneath an ornate stained-glass dome. (Henderson/Cremer Collection, ref. OH9405)

Left: A rare small window poster advertising the new Orient Line 'Orsova' class of first-class steamers travelling between Australia and England. An interesting feature is the mention of the newly invented wireless telegraphy at sea and the availability of single cabins. (Henderson/Cremer Collection, ref. OH10601)

Did You Know?

During a 1911 round trip to Australia on *Orsova* a baby girl was born. In honour of the ship, its nurse, the doctor, purser and captain the girl was named Orsova Nina Ingram Wilson Staunton Hodgson.

The function of a Royal Mail steamship was to maintain a regular, reliable, safe and speedy carriage of the mails between contracted routes throughout the Empire and the world. In this old photograph, bags of mail have been brought up on deck from down below, they were sorted into destinations, offloaded into express trains at the first practicable Australian port, usually Adelaide, and despatched to other states. It was the height of nineteenth- and twentieth-century logistics before the advent of the aircraft. (Henderson/Cremer Collection, ref. OH5950)

The following year *Ormuz* was again involved in an incident when she collided with HMS *Africa* in the English Channel. Luckily there was only minor damage and both ships were able to continue under their own steam.

In July 1907 it became clear that the Sir James Laing & Sons Australian service would never come to be, with the mail contract cancelled and the company eventually being forced into administration in 1908. The effect of this news was great, with newspaper reports suddenly much more sympathetic to the British shipping companies and their services, and a certain amount of shame

demonstrated for the way in which the contracts had previously been handled.

To deal with the immediate issue the Australian Government extended the Orient Line's existing contract until 31 January 1909. At the same time, they called for tenders for a new service to run for seven to ten years.

Orient Steam Navigation Company's agreement with the Royal Mail Steam Packet Company was already rocky by 1907, when they tendered for the new contract. Royal Mail tendered separately, without first consulting their partners. This did not pay off, with Orient Line once again being

Did You Know?

Early steamships did not have separate tables for dining. Instead there were long tables, around which all passengers of that class would be seated. Having a dining saloon fitted with 'restaurant style' arrangements was considered worthy of note in 1908.

Wireless Wonder

In 1910 *Otranto* made history when she sent a long-distance message via Marconi telegraph whilst at sea. *Otranto* was 321km north-west of Fremantle when she sent the message to HMS *Powerful* in Sydney Harbour, a distance of 3,218km. The wireless operator was Ernest Fisk, who later settled in Australia and was a foundation director of Amalgamated Wireless (Australasia) Ltd.

awarded the Australian Government mail contract in 1908. The new contract was not to take effect until February 1910, with the current terms once again extended. In effect, it was a weekly service alternating with P&O's British Government mail contract.

Royal Mail gave notice of their intention to withdraw from the partnership, with the termination to take effect in 1909 at the conclusion of the previously existing mail contract. The new contract provided a subsidy of £170,000 and a service time of twenty-six and a half days between Naples and Adelaide. In addition, Brisbane was added to the schedules and between February and May of each year the ships were to call at Hobart, Tasmania, on their return voyages to collect fruit cargo.

Without a running partner, Orient Steam Navigation Co. needed to quickly build a number of new ships to enable them to undertake the Australian mail contract on their own. It was determined that they needed five new 12,000-ton steamships to meet the requirements of the service. To fund the new-builds the directors pledged their personal credit.

The contracts for the new ships were given to four different shipbuilding companies, with the aim to get them all in service as quickly as possible.

All five ships, in addition to being approximately 12,000 tons, were to be twin-screw vessels with quadruple expansion engines, two funnels, two masts and fitted with Marconi telegraph. *Orsova*, which was built at John Brown & Co., and *Otway*, which was built at Fairfield Shipbuilding and Engineering Co., were both scheduled to be launched in November 1908.

Orsova, which was launched first, was fitted with 2,499 cubic metres of refrigerated cargo space and had capacity for more than 1,070 passengers. *Otway* was slightly smaller in dimensions but had $2,577\text{m}^3$ of refrigerated cargo space and could carry 1,095 passengers.

The following year, *Osterley* was launched at London & Glasgow Iron Shipbuilding Co. Unfortunately the event did not go off smoothly, with cold weather hardening the tallow, which had been used to grease the slipway, and *Osterley* getting stuck part of the way down.

Osterley was finally launched on 26 January, several days after the original attempt. *Otranto*, which was built by Workmen Clark and Co. of Belfast, suffered a similar fate when they attempted to launch her on 23 March. Her launch was not completed until 27 March 1909.

On 20 May *Orsova* was handed over to the Orient Line. Her maiden voyage to Australia departed on 25 June that year. *Otway* was the next to be completed, joining the Orient Line fleet on 29 May. She departed on 9 July on her maiden Australian voyage. *Osterley* was completed by 23 June and departed for Australia on 6 August.

On 6 July *Orvieto* was launched at Workmen Clark and Co., an event followed by the handing over of *Otranto* to Orient Line on 20 July.

Orvieto was handed over to Orient Line on 6 November. Just five days earlier the Russian steamer *Roman* had collided with *Osterley* while she was alongside in Port Said. Luckily the damage was not too severe and she was able to continue on her return journey to England that same evening.

With five new modern vessels in service Orient Line were able to retire the *Orient*. Now outdated and costly to run, *Orient* was sold for scrap. Orient Line were not to remain idle however, making the decision to continue to modernise their fleet. In February 1910 they issued a prospectus offering first mortgage debentures of £1,000, £500, £100 and £50. The aim was to raise £750,000 in capital to fund building new tonnage. This was not the first time that they had raised capital in such a way.

Seven ships were mortgaged to secure the debentures: *Orvieto*, *Osterley*, *Otranto*, *Orontes*, *Omrah*, *Ophir* and *Ormuz*. Having raised the needed capital, they were able to lay down a new ship at John Brown.

On 24 June 1911 *Otranto* and *Osterley* were present at the King George V Coronation Naval Review at Spithead.

A mere four days later *Orama* was launched at John Brown. Though they did not know it at the time, she was to be the last ship completed for Orient Line prior to the outbreak of World War I. The *Orama* was a triple-screw ship, the first of its type for Orient Line, and powered by a combination of both reciprocating engines and turbines.

She was handed over to Orient Line on 5 November; with a service speed of 18 knots and, at 12,927 tons, the largest Orient Liner yet built. She departed London on her maiden voyage on 10 November 1911, arriving in Fremantle on 12 December.

Ormuz was sold the following year to Compagnie de Navigation sud-Atlantique and went into service for her new owners under the name *Divona*. *Otranto* suffered a refrigeration break down that same year and a portion of her refrigerated cargo was lost.

As war drew ever closer, a new ship was laid down at the John Brown yard in May of 1913. Assigned the yard number 425, she was to be the first in the fleet to have geared turbines as her main engines and a cruiser-style stern. She was built on the slipway recently vacated by the Cunard liner *Aquitania* and for fifteen months work continued in a timely manner. With the outbreak of war however, that was all to change.

Did You Know?

Orotava inaugurated the Orient Line's service to the port of Brisbane on 2 September 1905. In honour of her arrival, a public holiday was declared in celebration.

The Great
Requisition

6

In early 1914, Orient Line's management was primarily concerned with the administration of its trust deed; in place to fund its aggressive shipbuilding schedule. This year saw the redemption of more than £11,000 of the debentures as well as a proposal to increase Orient Underwriting Fund's capital through the issue of additional shares.

But as the year marched on, the thoughts of the Orient managers turned to the increasingly hostile political climate gripping Europe, and as 1914 progressed the situation worsened.

A series of agreements and pacts between various European nations had led to a tangled web of alliances that served only to add tension to an otherwise uneasy peace between the various empires that dominated world affairs.

The British Government had been planning for a wartime scenario for some time. Already having the world's most respected and powerful navy at their disposal, for some time the government had been working with

Orama 1911–17 12,927grt. A wonderful image of the stylish *Orama* showing her low and lean look to great advantage. She was a magnificent ship and a modified version of the highly successful 1909 Orsova class. Sadly lost in World War I the *Orama* made only nine commercial mail voyages to Australia and carried 8,732 passengers. (Henderson/Cremer Collection, ref. 10006)

Orvieto 1909–31 12,130grt. *Orvieto* making a departure from Sydney as she passes Mrs Macquarie's Chair. (Henderson/Cremer Collection, ref. 10005)

Otranto 1909–18 12,124grt. *Otranto* running her speed trials off Skelmorlie on 1 July 1909, where she achieved, over two runs on the measured mile, a maximum speed of 18.95 knots. (Henderson/Cremer Collection, ref. OH6252)

Orontes 1902–22 9,023grt. August 1916 and the *Orontes* embarks Australian troops at Melbourne. *Orontes* had sailed from Sydney on 12 August and departed Melbourne on 16 August, calling at Adelaide and Fremantle and arriving at Plymouth on 2 October 1916. (Henderson/Cremer Collection, ref. OH11910)

Orama 1911–17 12,927grt. Requisitioned at the start of World War I as an armed merchant cruiser, the *Orama* is seen here in wartime colours and showing her starboard armament of 6in guns. (Henderson/Cremer Collection, ref. 10291)

Orvieto 1909–31 12,130grt. *Orvieto* was requisitioned by the Australian Government at the start of World War I as a troopship under pennant A3. In this role she was the flagship of the first convoy to leave Australia from Albany on 1 November 1914 for Egypt. (Pictures Collection, State Library Victoria)

shipping operators such as Orient Line to construct ocean-going liners to meet armed merchant cruiser specifications.

Design specifications meant that these ships could easily be called into service in a wartime capacity, with pre-allocated spaces for armaments to be installed. Furthermore, the increasing size and fast-paced introduction of ocean liners throughout the early part of the twentieth century meant that Britain would have a sizable fleet of troop transports at their disposal.

This planning was put into practice following the outbreak of World War I. What started in July 1914 as a series of declarations of war throughout continental Europe led to Britain's declaration of war against Germany on 4 August 1914. Within months, the war had escalated into one of the bloodiest and most deadly conflicts then recorded.

With Britain at war, other nations bound by the British Empire were also at war, and Australia was no exception.

Although an independent nation since 1901, King George V was the head of state in Australia and a large percentage of the population of the nation, as well as those in New Zealand, were British immigrants or descendants thereof.

Because of this, the declaration of war was met by a largely supportive public, with many men and boys volunteering to fight.

As expected, Orient Line was drawn into the conflict during its infancy, with the *Orvieto* being requisitioned by the Australian Government upon her August arrival in Sydney.

Ormonde 1917–52 14,852grt. *Ormonde* arriving in Sydney Harbour in February 1918. Laid down in October 1913 but not launched until early 1917, the *Ormonde* began life as a troop transport before being fitted out for the Australian Royal Mail service in 1919. (Henderson/Cremer Collection, ref. 10733)

Ormonde 1917–52 14,852grt. A magnificent starboard view of the *Ormonde* displaying her transitional styling and clearly showing the more amidships bridge. (Henderson/Cremer Collection, ref. 10700)

Osterley 1909–30 12,129grt. HMT *Osterley* anchored in New York Harbour on Armistice Day, 11 November 1918. The Great War had ended and to celebrate *Osterley* has been dressed overall in an array of flags rarely seen. (Henderson/Cremer Collection, ref. OH6163)

The 12,130-ton liner sat idle in Sydney for eight weeks before she was converted into a troop carrier. Following her conversion, she embarked over 1,300 troops and sailed for Egypt.

Otranto followed, being formally requisitioned on 4 August 1914. In fact, the Admiralty had originally requested *Otranto* for use as a hospital ship prior to the commencement of the war, but Orient had refused due to the ship's commitments on the Australian mail service.

In place of *Otranto*, Orient Line offered *Ophir* as a hospital ship, which the Admiralty accepted. After the outbreak of war there was no longer the option of refusal and the Admiralty called

Otranto into service, with the ship fitted out as an armed merchant cruiser.

Ophir had been under government control since July 1914, however she remained at anchor on the Thames for several weeks. Despite taking her up with the intention of using her as a hospital ship, the Admiralty ultimately placed *Ophir* into service as a mail transport. She sailed for Australia in October with mail and newspapers telling of a war that was gradually gripping the Continent.

Otway had also been requested for military use prior to the war and, as with *Otranto*, the Orient Line refused as the ship was occupied on the Australian Government mail contract. However, upon arrival in Gibraltar in August 1914 *Otway* was held at the port following Britain's declaration of war on Germany.

Having finally been released from Gibraltar, *Otway* made the journey to Australia. Upon her return to Britain, she was formally requisitioned for use as an armed merchant cruiser.

A rather shambolic fitting out took place at Tilbury, which saw the ship's entry into the Royal Navy delayed by several weeks. Many essentials were missing from the near-completed ship, and to make matters worse she had not been allocated a captain, meaning she could not sail. Eventually, *Otway* was completed, and with a captain assigned she joined the Tenth Cruiser Squadron at the end of November.

Orama was also requisitioned for an armed merchant cruiser role and by 12 September she was integrated into the Royal Navy. Her wartime service had a dramatic start when she went to the aid of a burning German cargo vessel, however upon arrival it became clear that the crew had purposefully scuttled their ship, which was a total loss.

In the early days of the war, *Omrah* remained in the Australian mail service, arriving in Brisbane during September 1914. Once alongside, the Australian Government requisitioned her for use as a troop transport.

Omrah's refurbishment was far less eventful than *Otway*'s, and she was ready to sail to Albany in Western Australia on 24 September. Here, she formed part of the large trooping movement congregating in that port,

taking Australian and New Zealander servicemen to the Middle East.

Orvieto was also involved in the movement of troops from Albany, on 1 November she departed the south-west Australian port bound for Suez. She sailed as the flagship of a convoy protected by the HMAS *Melbourne* and HMAS *Sydney*; two of Australia's most significant naval vessels, and once at sea the convoy was joined by the Imperial Japanese Navy's Battlecruiser *Ibuki*.

As *Orvieto*'s convoy was making way to the refuelling station in Colombo, Ceylon (now Sri Lanka), notice was received from the Australian radio station at the Cocos Islands that a German warship was approaching its position.

HMAS *Sydney* quickly responded, disabling the German ship, which by then had been identified as the cruiser *Emden*. HMAS *Sydney* carried her German crew to Colombo, where they were transferred to a number of vessels in the convoy including *Orvieto*. She received Prince Franz Joseph von Hohenzollern, a nephew of the Kaiser, who had been acting as *Emden*'s torpedo operator.

Orient Line had hoped to return *Orvieto* to civilian service in early 1915, however upon her return to Great Britain she was requisitioned by the Admiralty, this time as an armed merchant cruiser. The liner was refurbished at the Millwall Iron Works yard and entered service in her new role in March.

In February 1915 the *Omrah* was released from her wartime role and resumed passenger and mail services alongside her larger fleet mate *Osterley*.

Did You Know?

At the start of the war in October 1914 the 9,060-ton German steamer *Derfflinger* was captured off Egypt. She was renamed *Huntsgreen* and placed under the management of F. Green & Co. In 1917 she was transferred to Union-Castle management and then moved again in 1919 to Orient Line management until 1921.

Ophir left the Orient Line fleet in March of 1915, having been purchased by the Admiralty for £25,000 for use as an armed merchant cruiser.

As the Admiralty wanted to utilise the ship for an extended period, leasing the ship was cost prohibitive. *Ophir*'s long-term future in the Orient Line fleet had been under a cloud due to her higher than normal operating costs, and despite her popularity as the 'Queen of the Indian Ocean' the line were happy to accept the offer.

That same month, *Orama* was engaged in South Atlantic patrolling duties in search of the German cruiser *Dresden*. Sailing alongside the Monmouth Class armoured cruiser HMS *Kent*, the *Orama* was sent to Mas Afuera in the Juan Fernandez Islands, where *Dresden* was reportedly hiding. Here the two ships rendezvoused with the light cruiser HMS *Glasgow*.

Dresden was eventually located anchored in Cumberland Bay in Más a Tierra (now Robinson Crusoe Island). A short battle ensued, resulting in the scuttling of *Dresden,* whose captain came aboard HMS *Glasgow*. *Dresden*'s wounded crew were brought aboard *Orama*.

Otranto had been deployed to the Falkland Islands as a guard ship, while the Royal Navy searched for the *Dresden*. However, *Otranto*'s stay in the Falklands dragged on much longer than anticipated owing to the Admiralty being unwilling to relieve the ship until a replacement vessel arrived.

As such, the entire merchant crew of *Otranto* made it known that they would not re-sign unless allowed to return home, leading to the Admiralty eventually ordering the ship back to Great Britain in March 1915. Once alongside, her crew were paid off and released from service, while the ship was prepared for use in the armed merchant cruiser role.

That April the Admiralty requisitioned *Orsova* for use as a troop carrier. Initially, the ship was used on the Mediterranean service, taking British troops as far as Alexandria, Egypt. The following month, the ship was briefly returned to the Australian mail service, before being taken up by the Australian Government for her passenger capacity. In this role, *Orsova* carried Australian servicemen to Alexandria.

In June 1915, *Orama* made the long journey across the Pacific Ocean to Australia for a much-needed overhaul. The ship was accommodated at Sydney for her long refurbishment before returning to the South Atlantic in October.

Upon her return to the South Atlantic, *Orama* was patrolling near the Argentine–Uruguayan border, formed by the Río de la Plata, when the crew spotted the German vessel *President Mitre.* The crew of *Orama* was able to capture the German ship, claiming it for Great Britain.

As the war years dragged on, Orient Line settled into an uncomfortable new normality, operating a reduced mail service, while most of its fleet was occupied in support of the war effort.

One issue that occupied the minds of management during the 1916 board meeting was the painfully slow progress being made on the newest liner, *Ormonde*. Military contracts took precedence over civilian shipping and as such John Brown had been occupied with wartime work, leaving the *Ormonde*'s construction schedule in disarray.

Otway's year started with a notable mishap when she collided with the Dominion Line's SS *Dominion* near Birkenhead. Fortunately, the damage wasn't substantial and, as the *Otway* was en route to dry dock, repairs could be made without too great an inconvenience.

For much of the war the 1902-built *Orontes* had maintained the Australian mail service for Orient Line, however in 1916 she was called into military service for use as a troop transport. The 9,023-ton liner spent the remainder of the year carrying British and Australian troops to South Africa and the Middle East.

That May, the *Orvieto* completed her first government commission and was released back to Orient Line. However, her reprieve from wartime use was short-lived, with the ship called back into government service in July 1916. In her new role, *Orvieto* was used on patrols in the North Sea, intercepting non-British ships and directing them to pre-allocated ports, where exhaustive searches were conducted of their passenger and cargo complement.

Omrah was also called back into government service, being re-requisitioned in January 1917. She was used on the trooping service, transporting Australian servicemen to England. Later she was used under the Liner Requisition Scheme alongside the similarly requisitioned *Osterley*, operating a mandatory service for the government on the Australia to Great Britain run.

The completion of *Ormonde* should have been a joyous occasion for the Orient Line, however the newly finished ship was hastily completed as a troop carrier owing to the desperate need for military transports. She was sent on trooping services, carrying Australian, British and Indian troops between various ports in the Middle East.

Orsova hit a mine in the English Channel on 14 March 1917. The quick actions of her master saved the ship when he beached the vessel in Cawsand Bay near Plymouth Sound but unfortunately eight lives were lost.

She was later refloated and sent to the Devonport Naval Yard for repairs. However, the extent of the damage required specialist work, so after a quick patch up the ship travelled to Liverpool for a more permanent remedy.

The bravery of the crew in the face of such a dangerous incident was so great that several members were presented with special honours. This included the ship's chief officer, Lieutenant Commander Matheson, who was presented with a Distinguished Service Order, as well as second officer H. Watkins, who was awarded a Distinguished Service Cross.

Once in Liverpool the ship sat idle for well over a year, as naval work

Did You Know?

In 1919 the Allied Shipping Controller took charge of the surrendered German steamers, the 4,556-ton *Rio Negro*, the 4,588-ton *Rio Pardo* and the 8,332-ton *Friedrichsruhe*, all of which were placed under Orient Line management until 1921. The surrendered German steamer *Cordoba* was also allocated to Orient Line management in 1920.

took preference over the repairs to a civilian ship.

Orama remained in the South Atlantic, operating a patrol service. She was finally sent to Simonstown in South Africa in March 1917, where the ship was given a long overdue overhaul. The works took several months and when she returned to service she was ordered back to the United Kingdom via Canada.

While patrolling in Scottish waters on 22 July 1917, the *Otway* was sunk with the loss of ten lives after an attack by German U-boat *UC-49*. Following the attack, the U-boat surfaced nearby with the intention of taking *Otway*'s officers prisoner, however as the *Otway* sunk her forward guns fired unexpectedly, leading to the U-boat's hasty departure. The survivors were able to escape in *Otway*'s lifeboats and were later rescued by the Royal Navy.

From August, the *Orontes* saw service for the Ministry of War Transport under the Liner Requisition Scheme, operating between Liverpool and New York, while that same month *Orama* was sent to Liverpool for reconfiguration as a troop carrier.

Upon returning to military service, *Orama* performed convoy duties – a dangerous mission owing to the constant U-boat threat. She continued in this role until 19 October, when she was torpedoed by *U-62* while sailing off the Scilly Isles. The crippled ship could not be saved and the captain gave the order to abandon the vessel. All but fifty of the crew were evacuated and taken to the nearby American ships USS *Conyngham* and USS *Jacob James.*

However, those left behind were not forgotten, with the captain requesting the USS *Conyngham* to come alongside the stricken Orient Liner, so the remaining crew could evacuate. With the crew safely aboard the USS *Conyngham,* the drama looked to be subsiding. But a light was spotted aboard the ship, prompting the ship's master and a small search party to return to the ship once more and search the vessel. No one was found so the search party returned safely to the American ship, leaving *Orama* to founder.

For the Orient Line, the early years of 1918 were dominated by two major events; the first was the total requisition of their shipping fleet, with every express liner needed for military service.

The second major disruption was the gradual yet significant acquisition of Orient Line shares by its larger competitor P&O. During World War I the Green family decided to withdraw from shipping and instead pursue other interests. The firm of Gray Dawes, on behalf of Lord Inchcape, chairman of P&O, purchased shares from the Green family. The P&O shareholding in Orient Line grew to an ultimate holding of 51 per cent of the organisation this year, giving the company effective control of Orient Steam Navigation Co. and its operation.

A new company, Anderson, Green and Co., was created to manage the Orient Line, with the Anderson family still at the forefront of the management arrangement.

Despite this change in ownership, P&O and Orient Line would operate as separate companies under their own unique identities and house flags for decades to come.

Orient Line suffered further losses in May when *Omrah* was lost to a torpedo from *UB-52*. Such was the secrecy around wartime losses that no official notification was provided at the time, leading journalists to ask questions based on rumours of the ship's demise.

As the American involvement in the war peaked, several Orient liners found their way onto the North Atlantic run, transporting US troops to Europe, with *Osterley* and *Otranto* both sailing on this route from July 1918.

In September 1918, the *Orontes* and *Otranto* were both assigned to a particularly unfortunate convoy along with a number of other vessels from a range of shipping operators. Problems with the voyage began when a bout of Spanish influenza broke out aboard *Otranto*, and early in the voyage the ship collided with the French fishing vessel *Croisine*.

By 6 October, the convoy had made its way across the Atlantic, with land sighted as the ships approached the Isle of Islay. However, the vessels were sailing through a Force 11 storm, with damaging winds, heavy seas and poor visibility.

Suddenly, and without warning, the P&O vessel *Kashmir*'s steering gear failed, leading her to make a sharp turn into the side of the *Otranto*, badly damaging the Orient Line vessel.

Otranto was now in a dire situation, taking on water and adrift. The quick actions of the escort vessel HMS *Mounsey* led to the rescue of over 580 people from *Otranto*. Tragically more than 400 lives were lost, including *Otranto*'s captain. The ship was a total loss as the storm and violent seas drove her onto the rocky shores of Islay.

As the war entered its final months, *Orsova* was returned to wartime service, having finally been repaired from the damage caused by a mine in 1917. She was placed onto the North Atlantic service under the Liner Requisition Scheme.

On 11 November 1918 the bloody battles of World War I came to an end. With the signing of the Armistice many requisitioned ships were brought into British ports and prepared for repatriation voyages or refurbished and returned to their owners.

World War I had been brutal for Orient Line, with the loss of *Omrah*, *Otway*, *Otranto* and *Orama*. Added to the forced sale of *Ophir* to the government, Orient Line was left with just four large steamers to rebuild their Australian mail service. During the war the Orient liners had steamed a total of 534,792 miles, and carried 622,780 Allied troops and essential personnel and 15,000 prisoners-of-war.

Rebuilding
the Fleet

7

At the end of the war the Orient Line Australian mail service was in shambles and not able to resume until their ships were released from charter. In December 1918 *Orvieto* was released from government service and began a lengthy refurbishment, while *Orontes* and *Orsova* began the task of repatriating Australian soldiers.

In February and into March of 1919 *Ormonde* made a series of repatriation voyages between Egypt and Marseilles. She then sailed from Suez to Bombay, returning troops. In April she made voyages repatriating the wives and family of servicemen. *Ormonde* also made a voyage to the Russian port of Batoum with personnel and supplies for those fighting the Bolsheviks.

It was not until May that *Osterley* and *Ormonde* were released from government service and could commence refurbishment. Refurbishment was no easy feat in the months post-World War I. There were shortages of materials and labour, and thus it was not until October that the first ship back, *Orontes*, returned to Orient Line service. *Orsova*, *Orvieto* and *Ormonde* followed the following month and, together with the Australasian United Steam Navigation Co. ship *Indarra*, they were able to reinstate their Australian mail service.

Ormonde 1917–52 14,852grt. Unmistakably *Ormonde*, she had that special transitional look between the 1912 *Orama* and its successor *Orama II* of 1924. The first Orient liner with a cruiser stern and stovepipe funnels. (Henderson/Cremer Collection, ref. 10455)

Ormonde 1917–52 14,852grt. A typical Sydney departure showing *Ormonde* pulling away from the Company's old East Sydney Cove wharf, an area that now features high-rise apartments leading along a fashionable boardwalk to the Sydney Opera House. (Henderson/Cremer Collection, ref. OH6047)

Omar 1920–24 10,711grt. Formerly the German steamer *Königin Luise*, she was handed over to the British after World War I and subsequently managed and purchased by the Orient Line. Renamed *Omar*, she made eleven Australian voyages before being sold in 1924. (Henderson/Cremer Collection, ref. 40022)

Orcades 1921–27 9,764grt. A former German steamer, *Prinz Ludwig*. Built in 1914, was handed over to the British after World War I. Purchased by the Orient Line, she was renamed *Orcades* but only made five Australian voyages as she was not entirely suitable for the trade. (Pictures Collection, State Library Victoria)

Ormuz II 1921–27 14,588grt. Formerly the Nordeutscher Lloyd steamer *Zeppelin*, she was the most successful German steamer purchased by the Orient Line after World War I. Renamed *Ormuz*, she served with the Line until being sold in 1927. (Pictures Collection, State Library Victoria)

Orama II 1924–40 19,770grt. The first post-World War I new-build by the Orient Line. The *Orama* was for many years the fastest mail steamer on the Australian trade. *Orama* was the first passenger ship in the world to be fitted with gravity davits. (Henderson/Cremer Collection, ref. 10707)

Orama II 1924–40 19,770grt. The first ship in the famous 20,000-ton class of post-World War I ships built by the Orient Line, the *Orama* had the developing classic look so familiar with Orient ships. (Henderson/ Cremer Collection, ref. OH6183)

Orama II 1924-40 19,770grt. The first-class elegance of *Orama* with her finely figured wood panelling and the classically carved woodwork of the grand staircase. (Henderson/Cremer Collection, ref. folio 1_00253)

To supplement their mail service, Orient Line purchased three ships from the British Shipping Controller. All three of the ships purchased were former Norddeutscher Lloyd liners, the 1896 built *Königin Luise*, the 1906-built *Prinz Ludwig*, and *Zeppelin*, which was built in 1914. Both *Königin Luise* and *Prinz Lugwig* had run services to Australia under their German names whilst under ownership of the British Shipping Controller. *Königin Luise* was operated by Orient Line, *Prinz Ludwig* by P&O and *Zeppelin* was being managed by White Star Line.

Orient Line purchased *Königin Luise* in August 1920 and, after a round trip to Australia under her original name, renamed her *Omar*, replacing *Indarra*, which had proved unsuitable for Orient's Australian service. In March the following year Orient Line purchased the other two vessels, with *Prinz Ludwig* renamed *Orcades*, and *Zeppelin* renamed *Ormuz*.

In June of 1921 Orient Line began cruise voyages to Norway, reinstating a service that had ended with the outbreak of war in 1914, with *Ormuz* the first to depart.

The war had disrupted the mail service so thoroughly that Orient Line needed to renegotiate the mail contract with the Australian Government after the end of the war. The new contract was signed in September 1921 and called for a four-weekly mail service, with intermediate dispatches to Australia.

The new *Orcades* made her first voyage to Australia for Orient Line, departing on 8 October of that year,

and *Ormuz* followed, departing London on 12 November. *Omar* and *Orcades* were used for the intermediate Australian service, as both ships were too slow and too dated for both the main mail service and the premium passenger service.

In 1921 the Orient Line service was further shaken up by the Australian Navigation Act that resulted in the Line abandoning the practice of carrying passengers between Australian ports. The Navigation Act, which had been amended in 1920, had provisions that were designed to favour Australian coastal trade by Australian ships, by setting requirements for vessels travelling between Australian ports. These conditions made it impossible for the British shipping companies to continue their practice of offering short coastal voyages between Australian ports. This was a blow to Orient Line's finances as these routes had been popular and thus lucrative for the company.

As a consequence of the Australian Navigation Act, Orient Line vessels stopped calling at the port of Hobart, as they were not required to go there for the mail and there was no profit to be made by carrying passengers to and from the port. This created great difficulties for the port of Hobart, as not only did tourist traffic decline, but they were also provided with far fewer opportunities to export their fruit, with overseas lines no longer visiting. Orient Line did not accept their fate quietly however, continuing to petition

Did You Know?

On Christmas Eve 1927 *Osterley* was late departing Sydney when more than 100 crew members walked off the ship, refusing to take the liner to sea in a protest about the food aboard.

Orama II 1924–40 19,770grt. A marvellous
view of *Orama* making her departure
from Sydney. Before entering service as a
transport in World War II the *Orama* made
forty-five Australian mail voyages and
carried 32,414 passengers. (Henderson/
Cremer Collection, ref. OH6253)

Oronsay 1925–42 20,001grt. With the
flying debris of farewell streamers, the
Oronsay makes her way down Sydney
Harbour on another voyage back to
England. (Henderson/Cremer Collection,
ref. OH6246)

Oronsay 1925–42 20,001grt. The first Orient Line cruise from Sydney was by Oronsay in December 1932, Noumea was the only port of call. Oronsay is shown anchored in Noumea Harbour. She was opened for inspection, with the electric passenger lift the centre of visitors' attention. (Henderson/Cremer Collection, ref. 10475)

the Australian Government for both exemptions to and changes to the Act to allow them to perform coastal trade when they were in Australian waters.

Despite the downturn in Australian coastal trade, Orient Line were keen to both update and expand their Australian services. To this end they laid down three new ships. They received tenders from several shipbuilding companies for the new-builds and ultimately made what was to be a very successful partnership with one of the successful shipyards.

Post-World War I, Vickers Limited at Barrow-in-Furness had the capacity to take on new-builds. Despite having been largely focused on building warships in the past, they tendered for the Orient Line contracts and, with a low price and favourable terms, Orient accepted. They placed orders for two vessels with

Vickers and an order for a third to be built at John Brown & Co.

Orontes, which had been built in 1902, was now showing her age. The war years had not been kind to her and, as it was too costly to completely refit her, she was laid up in 1921. In 1922 she was sold for use as a floating exhibition centre, but the purchaser, the British World Trade Exhibition Co., went into receivership and as a result Orontes remained in the Orient fleet until 1926, when she was finally sold for scrap.

In November 1922 the Orvieto was issued a special licence to enable her to transport passengers in Australian coastal trade. This licence granted Orvieto the right to convey passengers from Sydney to Melbourne for the Melbourne Cup. Unfortunately, not everyone was happy about these arrangements. The dispute

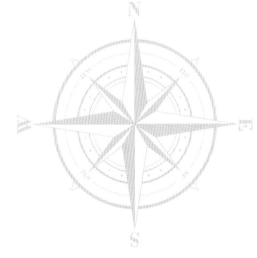

Otranto II 1926–57 20,032grt. *Otranto* captured by the lens in Sydney Harbour. A long-serving ship, *Otranto* made sixty-eight mail voyages to Australia, carrying some 63,000 passengers during her thirty-one-year career. (Henderson/Cremer Collection, ref. 10771)

began among the firemen but quickly spread, with crew refusing to work and *Orvieto* delayed in Melbourne. The strike action resulted in the arrest of 161 stewards, cooks and pantrymen on 14 November, with the crew ordered back to the ship. This had the effect of discouraging Orient Line from seeking further special licences.

Labour disputes were not limited to Australian waters, however, with delays reported at the British shipbuilders as well in 1923. This slowed the completion of the new Orient liners.

In April of that year it was announced by Orient Line that they would not have second class on board their new vessels. The new ships were to be built as two-class, with only first- and third-class areas on board. That month, *Ormonde* was sent to John Brown & Co. for conversion to an oil-burning vessel and at the same time they reconfigured her accommodation, removing second class.

On 16 March 1924, *Omar* arrived in Fremantle port three days after she was due, owing to a number of circumstances, including bad weather in the Bay of Biscay and traffic conditions at the entrance to the Suez Canal. The worst of the circumstances, however, was the loss of a propeller in the Indian Ocean on 10 March. This, of course, meant that the ship could not travel at her full speed and it also resulted in the ship taking on some water in the aft hold. She was nonetheless able to continue on her way under her own steam, though the ship's personnel were drilled thoroughly in lifeboat exercises

for the remainder of the voyage, in case of further mishap.

At Vickers Ltd the first Orient Line ship to be built at that yard was taking shape and on 20 May she was ready for launch. *Orama* was named for the earlier liner lost in World War I, and was launched by Miss Winifred Cook, daughter of the High Commissioner for Australia. It was a grand event with big crowds turning out to see the ship take to the water for the first time.

Less than two months later *Omar* left the fleet, sold to the SS Byron Co. on 4 July 1924. She was soon to be replaced in the Orient Line fold by the *Oronsay*, which was launched at John Brown & Co. Clydebank on 14 August. Christened by Viscountess Novar, at the time of her launch she was the largest ship to be launched on the Clyde in two years.

Both *Orama* and *Oronsay* were twin-screw ships. *Orama* was powered by six single-reduction geared turbines, while *Oronsay* had two Brown-Curtis high-reduction geared turbines. Both ships would prove to be fast, with service speeds of around 20 knots.

On 15 November, *Orama* set sail on her maiden Australian voyage. She arrived in Fremantle on 10 December 1924. *Orama* was the first ship to be fitted with the new Welin-MacLachlan davit to carry her lifeboats. The new davit offered a serious improvement in safety and allowed lifeboats to be filled and lowered in minutes. This style of davit, known as a gravity davit, is still used today.

Otranto II 1926–57 20,032grt. The elegance of the 20,000-ton-class of Orient Line ships is personified in this image of the *Otranto*'s first-class lounge. A combination of ivory and blue, along with the ornately subdued plaster work, parquet floors and natural light, made for comforting travel. (Henderson/Cremer Collection, ref. folio 1_00289)

Did You Know?

Orford's maiden arrival in Sydney Harbour occurred on 22 November 1928, just as construction began on the Sydney Harbour Bridge arch.

Oronsay was delivered early the following year and her maiden voyage to Australia departed on 7 February 1925. *Oronsay* had been fitted with a number of new finishes, including plastic sheeting glued to her bulkheads, to make them easy to clean. Unfortunately, the new materials were not without issues, with the panels cracking with a loud noise during testing of the heating system prior to completion. As a result, these fittings needed to be replaced, which took extra time and expense.

Orient Line launched another new liner at the Vickers yard in 1925. *Otranto* was built along similar lines to her previous two sister ships and was christened by Mrs Amery, the wife of the Secretary of State for the Colonies, on 9 June.

With new tonnage coming into the fleet, Orient Line retired a further two ships, with *Orcades* sold to the breakers on 30 March 1925 and *Orontes* finally leaving the fleet in 1926.

Otranto's left London on her maiden voyage to Australia on 9 January 1926, travelling via Gibraltar, Toulon, Naples, Suez, Aden and Colombo. The following month, *Orama* inaugurated regular calls by the Orient fleet at Southampton.

Otranto II 1926–57 20,032grt. Many an Orient Line United Kingdom cruise departed from Immingham. In this image the *Otranto* is alongside and her stewards wait to assist passengers and their baggage from the train to the ship before *Otranto* departs for a summer cruise to Norway. (Henderson/Cremer Collection, ref. P&O_247)

Did You Know?

The famous English novelist D.H. Lawrence travelled to Australia on the Orient Liner *Orsova* in 1922. Once there he stayed at Thirroul, rented a house named 'Wyework' and wrote the novel *Kangaroo*.

On 11 May, during a month-long Mediterranean cruise, *Otranto* suffered damage to her port bow and side when she struck cliffs off Greece while sailing at night in bad weather. The sky was obscured and lights were not visible, resulting in the crash, and though the damage was bad, she was still able to make Piraeus under her own steam. In early June she returned to Southampton for permanent repairs. This meant that she did not depart on her second Australian voyage until 18 September.

Ormuz was sold to her original owners, Norddeutscher Lloyd Line, on 22 April 1927. She was renamed *Dresden* and entered the Atlantic service for the German line.

Later that year, *Orford* was launched at Vickers by Lady Ryrie, the wife of the Australian High Commissioner. The ship's build had been significantly delayed by a coal strike and she did not take to the water for the first time until 27 September 1927.

Orford's maiden voyage was a twenty-eight-day Mediterranean cruise, which departed Southampton on 13 April 1928. *Otranto* joined *Orford* in being employed in Norwegian cruises during the 1928 summer season and on 11 August was involved in a collision with the 8,000-ton Japanese vessel

Otranto II 1926–57 20,032grt. *Otranto*, photographed from an unusual angle in Sydney Harbour in 1931. (Henderson/ Cremer Collection, ref. 10766)

Otranto II 1926–57 20,032grt. *Otranto* was built to carry 572 passengers in the first saloon and 1,168 in the third class. This view is of the third-class dining room. (Henderson/Cremer Collection, ref. 10568)

Above: *Orford* 1928–40 19,941grt. A wonderful view of *Orford* in Sydney Harbour. Of the five 20,000-ton sisters, the *Orford* arguably held the role as the most popular ship for cruising, particularly from Britain. (Henderson/Cremer Collection, ref. OH10751)

Above right: *Orford* 1928–40 19,941grt. An imposing starboard view of *Orford* preparing to come alongside. A very popular ship, the *Orford* made twenty-four mail voyages on the Australian service and carried 12,848 passengers before her unfortunate loss in World War II. (Henderson/Cremer Collection, ref. OH6207)

Kitano Maru. Over the course of three court hearings in the Admiralty Court, Court of Appeal and the House of Lords, the blame was shifted between the two companies, before it was determined that both ships were responsible for the incident.

Though *Otranto* was taken out of service for repairs, *Orford* continued to operate cruises until 13 October, when she departed on her maiden voyage to Australia. She arrived in Australia in November 1928.

That same month, *Osterley* was called to the aid of a German training ship, *Pommern*. The barque was in distress owing to a severe storm with gale force winds, which had caused both foremast and mainmast to collapse. The ship had also lost her wireless. The Bremen steamer *Rhoen* was standing by and was able to radio for aid. A tug, *Heros*, arrived on the scene and later three steamships, *Osterley*, *Lancastria* and *Matiana*, came to the aid of the stricken vessel.

The seas were so bad that no lifeboats could be launched. The tug was eventually able to get a line across to the *Pommern*, while the *Osterley*, *Lancastria* and *Matiana* shone lights on the scene. The crew of the *Pommern* were rescued and taken aboard the *Heros*, however the storm caused damage to *Osterley* as she was departing the scene.

Orford 1928–40 19,941grt. The understated elegance of *Orford*'s first-class café; simple extravagance was the byword in the decoration of the Orient Line 20,000-ton ships built in the 1920s. (Henderson/Cremer Collection, ref. 10421)

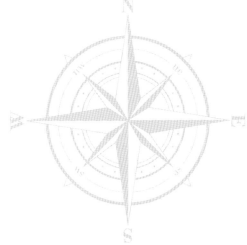

Orontes II 1929–62 19,970grt. An official company postcard view of *Orontes*, the last Orient liner to sail with the old black-hull livery. (Henderson/Cremer Collection, ref. 10500)

Orvieto 1909–31 12,130grt. Anniversary Day 26 January 1926, with *Orvieto* anchored in the stream as flagship for the traditional Sydney Regatta races, held on what is now called Australia Day. (Henderson/Cremer Collection, ref. 40036)

8

The Great Depression

Orient Line launched another new vessel at Vickers-Armstrongs on 26 February 1929. The new ship was called *Orontes* and she was christened by Lady Anderson, wife of the chairman, in front of a large crowd. The new ship was the first in the Orient fleet to have a raked bow and it was a striking change to the forward profile, making *Orontes* instantly recognisable. She was moved to the fitting-out basin, where she was given accommodation for 508 first-class passengers and 1,112 third-class passengers.

Her fitting out was completed in early September of that year and before she had even completed a shakedown cruise she was chartered, along with *Orford*, to be an official ship of the Schneider Trophy for the Royal Aero Club. Just over a week later she departed Southampton

Orsova 1909–36 12,036grt. 26 January 1929 and *Orsova* takes centre stage on Sydney Harbour as Anniversary Day Regatta flagship, leaning to a typical Sydney Southerly Buster. (Henderson/Cremer Collection, ref. OH6054)

The Australian cricket team were regular travellers by Orient Line on their way to and from England. Nets were put up along one side of the boat deck for regular practice or games against a passengers' team. (Henderson/Cremer Collection, ref. 11243)

on her shakedown cruise, before being made ready for her maiden voyage to Australia. She arrived in Fremantle on 25 November 1929.

The good times were not to last. The Great Depression was taking hold and affecting trade in both Britain and Australia.

In late 1929 *Osterley* was withdrawn from service and laid up at the end of a return voyage from Australia. She was outdated and outclassed by the new ships that Orient was bringing into service. In March 1930 *Osterley* was sold to P&W MacLellan of Glasgow to be broken up.

With profits falling, *Orvieto* was withdrawn from service and laid up in Southampton in October 1930, following *Osterley* to the shipbreakers in March 1931.

In the minutes of the annual general meeting held on 19 December 1930 it was noted that:

In view of the economic difficulties of Australia, we must expect a serious reduction in our revenue for the next few years, and we are confident that our Shareholders will support us in conserving the liquid resources of the Company by a sharp reduction in dividend.

Orsova and Ormonde, now the two oldest ships in the fleet, were converted to single-tourist-class ships in 1931, with Orsova arriving in Australia in June and Ormonde in December 1931 for the first time in their new configurations. The new layout greatly reduced the passenger capacity of both ships but provided much more comfortable accommodation for those aboard.

On 19 March 1932 Australia celebrated an iconic event, with the opening of the Sydney Harbour Bridge. Orford was in Sydney for the occasion and carried representatives of the New South Wales agricultural committees. The invited guests watched from the decks of the ship as P&O's Maloja led the procession of ships. Orford was the second to pass under the completed bridge. Orford was followed by the Koninklijke Paketvaart-Maatschappij ship Nieuw Zeeland and the Adelaide Steamship Company's Manunda. The clearance at high tide was a mere 2.43m between the top of Orford's mast and the Harbour Bridge.

In January 1933 Orient Line introduced a call at Palma, Majorca, on voyages to and from Australia. Not only did this add a destination of interest to those travelling between Britain and Australia, it also allowed the Orient ships to carry tourists to the island from Britain and develop holiday packages. Those tourists could holiday on Majorca and return home on the next Orient Line ship to call at the port. Orient undertook further cruising itineraries, with Orontes in 1933 offering a six-week cruise to the West Indies.

In 1934, with the effects of the Great Depression starting to ease, there was a new Orient Line ship launched at Vickers-Armstrongs. The company had become the preferred builder of Orient vessels. In the ten years since the first Orient ship built at their yard had launched they had built four of the company's five new ships.

On 7 December Orion was launched at Barrow-in-Furness. It was a highly publicised launch, owing to the ship being named and launched by HRH the Duke of Gloucester (Prince Henry) who was in Australia at the time. Before launching the ship he said:

> Before performing this act of magic which will cause this beautiful ship to take the water so many miles away, I send a greeting to my countrymen in Barrow-in-Furness who are so fortunate as to be present at her launching.

The launch itself was performed by radio, with the Duke activating a switch at the Brisbane Town Hall that caused the ship to take to the water for the first time.

Orion was a very different ship to the liners that had come before her. The design work was overseen by Colin

AUSTRALIAN XI
ENGLISH TOUR
1930

With the compliments of the
ORIENT LINE

Orient Line ships regularly carried both the Australian and English cricket XIs on their travels to battle for the Ashes. The teams practised on deck and played matches ashore at ports of call. Signed by Australian star Don Bradman, this brochure from the collection was produced by the line to celebrate the 1930 tour. (Henderson/Cremer Collection, images ref. P&O_091 and ref. OH9430)

Orama II 1924–40 19,770grt. *Orama* striking a pose against the backdrop of the building of Sydney Harbour Bridge. This photograph was taken in the week the arches of the bridge were joined. (Henderson/Cremer Collection, ref. 10393)

Sydney Harbour Cruise

Whilst cruising Sydney Harbour, before passing under the completed bridge for the first time, the invited guests on board *Orford* were entertained by Tooth's Brewery Band. The band was quickstep champion of the Commonwealth in 1930 and 1931 and runner-up in 1932.

Anderson, junior partner of Anderson, Green & Co. and Brian O'Rorke, a New Zealand architect. The two men created an interior design that celebrated the feel of being on a ship, rather than trying to conceal it. The older ships had tended to follow the design style of a country house at sea. *Orion* was a ship and proud of it.

Her interiors were art deco with plastics and Australian woods used throughout. Furniture, fittings and even dining sets were all different from the ships of the past. The first-class dining room was air-conditioned, as were some of her cabins, *Orion* being the first British ship to have an air conditioning plant. She was also the first British passenger ship to be fitted with a sprinkler system for use in case of fire. Fourteen of her two-berth first-class cabins had two big beds and some of the special staterooms had windows rather than portholes.

Orion commenced her shakedown cruise in the Mediterranean on 14 August 1935. During the cruise, she received a distress call from the Cunard-White Star ship *Doric*, whilst navigating in heavy fog on 5 September. *Orion* and P&O's *Viceroy of India* were able to come to *Doric*'s aid, with *Orion* taking aboard 686 of *Doric*'s passengers and forty-two of her crew.

It was not just *Orion*'s interiors that were different. *Orion* entered service with a corn-coloured hull and a single funnel and mast. This was a departure from the previous 20,000-ton ships, which had required two funnels to deal with the engine exhaust. Engineering advances had allowed *Orion* to use only one funnel, which gave her a very distinctive profile. The corn-coloured hull was designed to appeal to the public, who had favoured the lighter colour when it was tested on *Orama*. It had the added bonus of helping to deflect the sun's heat from the ship, especially important when travelling in the tropics.

Orion arrived in Fremantle on her maiden voyage on 29 October 1935. At the same time as *Orion* entered service, Orient Line made the decision to convert all third-class accommodation in their fleet to tourist class.

In 1936 *Orama* was sent for refit at Vickers-Armstrongs. With the refit

Ormonde 1917–52 14,852grt. A stern view of *Ormonde* as the regatta flagship on Anniversary Day in Sydney 1931. Sydney Harbour ferries plied to and from Circular Quay with a constant stream of visitors to enjoy the delights of refreshments on board and have a grandstand view of the yacht races. (Henderson/Cremer Collection, ref. OH6241)

Orion 1935–63 23,371grt. *Orion* on her sensational maiden arrival at Sydney in 1935, showing her original funnel before it was made taller. (Henderson/Cremer Collection, ref. 10813)

Oronsay 1925–42 20,001grt. A wonderful 1931 image of *Oronsay* at the head of Farm Cove in Sydney. She is being moved with the assistance of tugs from her Woolloomooloo berth to Sydney Cove. (Henderson/Cremer Collection, ref. OH8525)

Orion 1935–63 23,371grt. Alongside at the Farm Cove Finger Wharf Woolloomooloo in Sydney, with *Otranto*'s funnels in the background. (Henderson/Cremer Collection, ref. OH6104)

Orion 1935–63 23,371grt. Uncluttered, modern, art deco, simple, functional, were all the words and many more used to describe *Orion* – she was just so different and exciting, exemplified in this image of her first-class lounge. (Henderson/Cremer Collection, ref. P&O_053)

Orion 1935–63 23,371grt. The effective simplicity of the main staircase, functional and easily maintained. Throughout *Orion* the calming effect of timber was used to great effect. Sycamore and Australian timbers such as jarrah, myrtle and maple were used extensively. (Henderson/Cremer Collection, ref. 10743)

Did You Know? ✈

Orama was the first Orient liner to be painted with the corn-coloured hull. She was painted in 1934 to test public opinion, with the colour being returned to its original look after two voyages. She was repainted in the corn colour in 1935.

completed she left Barrow-in-Furness, returning to London to be prepared for her next passenger voyage. On 25 April she was involved in a collision, when she was rammed by the Yugoslav vessel *Sveti Duje*. The smaller *Sveti Duje* was badly damaged, but the damage to *Orama* was luckily fairly limited. Both ships were able to make way under their own power and *Orama* was quickly repaired and able to re-enter service on schedule.

In August 1936, *Orsova* made her final call to Australia. Whilst in Melbourne on 17 August, Miss Orsova Nina Hodgson, the girl who had been born on the ship's maiden voyage, and her mother were invited aboard as guests as part of the farewell celebration. After arriving back in London, *Orsova* was sold to the shipbreakers, departing the fleet in October 1936. *Orsova* was the last of the pre-World War I ships to leave the Orient fleet.

Orford 1928–40 19,941grt. Opening day of the Sydney Harbour Bridge and *Orford* is about to pass beneath it as she takes part in the procession of ships on 19 March 1932. (Henderson/Cremer Collection, ref. P&O_445)

Orion 1935–63 23,371grt. A company-issued postcard view of *Orion* showing the heightened funnel. (Henderson/Cremer Collection, ref. 10449)

Did You Know?

On 31 May 1936, *Orford* embarked Emperor Haile Selassie of Ethiopia in Gibraltar, carrying him to England, where he was to spend the next five years in exile.

Orion 1935–63 23,371grt. *Orion* coming out of her Woolloomooloo Finger Wharf berth at Sydney, leaving her running mate *Otranto* still alongside. (Henderson/Cremer Collection, ref. 10893)

Above: The most sought-after invitation in town. *Orford* was second in line of steamships in procession in the harbour as part of the celebrations on the opening day of the Sydney Harbour Bridge in March 1932. Guests were entertained to lunch and to music by Tooth's Brewery's award-winning band. (Henderson/Cremer Collection, ref. OH5900)

Oronsay 1925–42 20,001grt. In the days before cruise ships had portable pontoons, passengers at ports where the ship could not go alongside would descend the sometimes swaying gangplank lowered over the side of the ship into the waiting launches below. (Henderson/Cremer Collection, ref. 11175)

Orion 1935–63 23,371grt. This 7 November 1935 image shows *Orion* being edged alongside at the Woolloomooloo Finger Wharf at Sydney with the old 1909 *Orsova* already alongside. (Henderson/Cremer Collection, ref. 10923)

Orion 1935–63 23,371grt. A classic view of a vanished era: *Orion* alongside the old passenger terminal on the West Side of Sydney's Circular Quay. (Henderson/Cremer Collection, ref. 10451)

Did You Know?

Orford's sports deck had two tennis courts in addition to courts for other shipboard games.

Left: *Orion* 1935–63 23,371grt. *Orion* passing under the Sydney Harbour Bridge. (Henderson/Cremer Collection, ref. 10452)

Below left: *Orcades II* 1937–42 23,456grt. Sister ship to *Orion*, the *Orcades* takes to the water at Barrow-in-Furness on 1 December 1936. She was built in the yards of Vickers-Armstrong Ltd, in the days when great ships were constructed on slipways surrounded by gantries. (Henderson/Cremer Collection, ref. 10399)

Above: *Orcades II* 1937–42 23,456grt. A dramatic image of *Orcades* as she arrives in Sydney for the first time on 15 November 1937. (Henderson/Cremer Collection, ref. 10886)

Orcades II 1937–42 23,456grt. The openness of the first-class boat (games) deck was a far cry from earlier ships where passengers vied with ship's machinery for space. On *Orcades* both ship and passenger requirements met without any fuss. (Henderson/Cremer Collection, ref. 10404)

Orcades II 1937–42 23,456grt. The pool tavern was one of the many genius rooms that were built as a result of the collaboration of Colin Anderson and Brian O'Rorke and was eminently suitable for its purpose. It featured folding doors that opened to the pool, stainless steel, aluminium-framed chairs, chrome, bakelite, vinyl flooring and coverings, and cleanable painted columns. Very art deco and very functional. (Henderson/Cremer Collection, ref. 10939)

Orcades II 1937–42 23,456grt. Catching the early morning sunrise in Sydney Harbour, another fine view of the *Orcades*. (Henderson/Cremer Collection, ref. 10822)

Orcades II 1937–42 23,456grt. The first-class lounge epitomised the designers' mantra that the public spaces should be primarily comfortable, not hide the fact that you are at sea and provide an endless atmosphere of enjoyment. (Henderson/Cremer Collection, ref. 10948)

Did You Know?

Orontes had a special nursery and nursery dining room. Children were allowed to share the sports deck with adults.

Orama II 1924–40 19,770grt. A sign of things to come. In 1934 the *Orama* made two Australian voyages sporting a new experimental livery of a corn-coloured hull, which was a huge success and all new-builds starting with the *Orion* adopted the new colour scheme. (Henderson/Cremer Collection, ref. 10753)

Oronsay 1925–42 20,001grt. *Oronsay* on a cruise from Sydney to New Zealand in 1937. Orient Line ships were known for their broad-shaded promenade decks, it was a deliberate design feature echoing the familiar Australian Verandah. (Henderson/Cremer Collection, ref. 11172)

Opposite: *Oronsay* 1925–42 20,001grt. Hair nets, hats, a smile and a good book, Cruising was one of *Oronsay*'s popular pastimes in Australian waters during the 1930s, as seen here on a South Sea Island cruise to Fiji in 1938. (Henderson/Cremer Collection, ref. 10986)

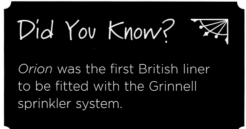

R.M.S. ORONSAY.
PASSING UNDER THE HARBOR BRIDGE
SYDNEY. N.S.W.

Oronsay 1925–42 20,001grt. An early
morning Sydney arrival, *Oronsay* makes her
way under the Harbour Bridge to her berth
at Pyrmont. (Henderson/Cremer Collection,
ref. P&O_333)

Did You Know?

Orion was the first British liner
to be fitted with the Grinnell
sprinkler system.

On 23 September of that year the officers and crew of *Ormonde*, together with four firemen from Sydney, spent four hours battling a fire on board the liner whilst she was off the New South Wales coast at Eden. The fire had broken out in one of the cargo holds and the ship put in at Twofold Bay in order to bring the blaze under control. A fire truck was dispatched from Sydney to assist in the efforts and firefighting foam was used to help extinguish the flames.

As the year came to a close a new ship was being built at Vickers-Armstrongs. The *Orcades* was launched by Mrs I.C. Geddes, wife of the chairman of Anderson, Green & Co. Her launch was accomplished on 1 December 1936 but things did not go smoothly. There were strong winds blowing from the north-west on the day of launch and it made the hull difficult to control. As a result it was decided to tow *Orcades* to a deep-water berth in the channel, rather than the dock. Whilst under tow *Orcades* hit an old wooden pier, breaking off 6m of the pier. The ship was aground for an hour before she could be freed.

Orcades was similar in design to the *Orion*. She was a twin-screw ship with six Parsons-type geared steam turbines,

Orontes II 1929–62 19,970grt. A superb view of the *Orontes* sailing from the old Finger Wharf at Woolloomooloo on 7 November 1931, Sydney, at the start of a voyage to London, whilst her sister ship *Otranto II* prepares to sail on the same day for Brisbane. (Henderson/Cremer Collection, ref. OH6107)

Orsova 1909–36 12,036grt. A view of *Orsova*'s final departure from Melbourne in 1936, being farewelled by well-wishers including a dog and a cockatoo. (Henderson/Cremer Collection, ref. 10544)

and she had a service speed of about 20 knots. She was fitted with 5,895m^3 of refrigerated cargo space. Fitting out was to take seven months.

In May 1937, King George VI's Coronation Naval Review took place. *Otranto* was present for the event, carrying paying passengers in a one-class configuration.

Two months later, in mid-July, *Orcades* was delivered to the Orient Line. She departed Southampton on a three-week Mediterranean cruise on 21 August, calling at Capri, Kotor, Dubrovnik, Istanbul and Palermo. On 9 October she departed on her maiden voyage to Australia.

She followed up her maiden Australian voyage with two more round trips, before undertaking a series of cruises to northern Europe. After another two round Australian trips and a further cruise she arrived back in Southampton on 12 May 1939 suffering engine problems. She had been due to undertake more cruises, but it was decided to cancel them, and *Orcades* was sent back to her builders for refit.

Otranto II 1926–57 20,032grt. *Otranto* passing the Royal Australian Navy base at Garden Island as she enters Farm Cove in Sydney heading to her berth at the Woolloomooloo Finger Wharf. (Henderson/ Cremer Collection, ref. OH8503)

A Second Global War

9

On 1 September 1939, Nazi Germany invaded Poland, effectively starting World War II. Britain and France's declaration of war on Germany on 3 September led to an escalation of military preparedness that, for Britain, meant activating a fleet of requisitioned liners that exceeded what was used during World War I.

At the outbreak of war, the 1924-built *Orama* was en-route to England having just called at Colombo. However, the beginning of hostilities led to an unexpected rerouting via Cape Town in order to avoid the Mediterranean Sea. The additional mileage led to the ship's return being severely delayed, with her not arriving back in Great Britain until mid-October.

As with World War I, Britain's entry into war led to the immediate declaration of war by both Australia and New Zealand.

Australians learnt of their new wartime status on the evening of 3 September when Prime Minister Robert Menzies made a lengthy radio broadcast to the public. That same day, New Zealand declared war on Germany, which was officially confirmed by the Acting Prime Minister Peter Fraser.

On 3 September *Otranto* was berthed in Sydney Harbour following a cruise to Fiji. With Australia at war she was quickly called up for service, charged with transporting Australian troops to Great Britain. *Orcades*, *Orford* and *Orion* were all in British waters and quickly pushed into wartime service, with the three ships sailing in a convoy to Alexandria, Egypt, with full complements of troops.

Once back in British waters, *Orion* was released to Orient Line. But she was called back into government service on 22 October, this time as a requisitioned liner for a government-controlled passenger voyage to Sydney. Meanwhile, the *Orontes* was left in Orient Line's charge, operating a voyage to Brisbane with a full passenger list. Her return service had a much-diminished passenger complement; however her stores were full to the brim with a valuable cargo of food to support the war effort.

Ormonde saw service in both world wars. She was called up in November 1939 and, following conversion, she entered wartime service on the Canadian run that December. In this role she carried Canadian troops from Halifax to Greenock, Scotland.

In early December, *Orion* made an Orient Line passenger voyage to Sydney, but upon her arrival she was taken to the dry dock and converted for trooping use. Later that month, *Orama* joined *Ormonde* on the Canadian service.

At the Orient Line's annual general meeting on 20 December 1940 the perils of war and the disturbance that government requisitions made to the mail contract were discussed, with it being noted that:

Since the outbreak of war the regularity of our sailings under the Mail Contract with the Government of the Commonwealth of Australia has been disturbed.

In early 1940 *Orcades, Otranto, Orion* and *Orford* were all assigned to convoy duties on the Australian trooping service. This role saw the ships deliver troops to Egypt, before making various onward voyages in support of Allied trooping movements.

For the next few months, *Otranto* and *Orford* operated in close quarters, both being sent to Marseilles, France, before sailing together to Toamasina, Madagascar. Having embarked troops there, the two ships sailed north to Mombasa, Kenya, where they expected to receive onward orders to their ultimate destination.

Upon their arrival in the Kenyan port, there were no additional instructions for the ships, resulting in their captains opting to sail to Port Said, Egypt, where many troop convoys were being deployed.

On arrival in Port Said, both the British and French authorities had no additional orders for the ships, but after a lengthy delay they eventually received orders to proceed to Toulon, France.

In order to make the passage through the Mediterranean, both *Orford* and *Otranto* were officially loaned to the French military as troop transports. However, neither the captain of the *Orford* nor his counterpart on *Otranto* had any intention of sailing unprotected. They requested a military escort and received support from the French Navy.

Their voyage to Toulon was routed via Malta, however as the liners approached

Orcades II 1937–42 23,456grt. Another view of *Orcades* in Sydney Harbour. She was exceptional, outstanding in design and destined for a short but brilliant career. (Henderson/Cremer Collection, ref. 10777)

Orcades II 1937–42 23,456grt. A classic starboard view of *Orcades* in Port Philip Bay in 1938. She was a remarkable ship with a short five-year career during which she made only eight mail voyages to Australia carrying 5,060 passengers. (Pictures Collection, State Library Victoria)

the British-controlled island, they were ordered away, so proceeded in haste towards France under the protection of the Guépard-class destroyer *Lion*. The ships eventually arrived in Toulon, where they were abruptly ordered to sail for Marseilles.

Berthing space was at a premium in Marseilles, so while *Otranto* received a landside berth, the *Orford* was ordered to an anchorage point outside the protection of the port's anti-aircraft artillery, despite protests from her captain.

On 1 June 1940 during the evacuation of France, German bombers attacked the *Orford*. The ship took heavy damage and risked becoming a wreck in the port, which would have caused difficulties for the evacuation. As a result the French authorities ordered her to be beached.

However, *Orford* was now a dead ship with total power loss, meaning she was not manoeuvrable, nor could her anchor be raised. A combination of quick actions from the port's tugboat operators and the cutting of *Orford*'s anchor chains allowed her to be manoeuvred into a safe location, and she was run aground, where she burnt out. Later, her hull bottom was dynamited to ensure she would not drift off.

Orford's captain along with her crew members made their escape

Orcades II 1937–42 23,456grt. Shown rounding Bennelong Point in Sydney Harbour, now the site of the Sydney Opera House. In her brief two years of passenger service the *Orcades* established an instant popularity that was sadly cut short when she was lost to a German submarine in the South Atlantic in World War II. (Henderson/Cremer Collection, ref. 10806)

from Marseilles just before it fell into enemy hands. After the war *Orford* was refloated in 1947 and taken for breaking up at Savona in Italy.

On 2 January 1940 *Orion* departed Sydney Harbour with a group of Australian troops aboard. After transiting the Tasman Sea, the ship arrived in Wellington, New Zealand, four days later. There she embarked New Zealand personnel before joining her fleet mate *Orcades* in a convoy bound for Egypt.

That same month, *Orontes* arrived in Australia at the end of a mail run. Upon her return to Great Britain she was requisitioned for use as a troop carrier.

Orama was also engaged in government service, however rather than carrying troops she was used as a requisitioned liner, departing for Australia in this role on 10 February 1940. *Ormonde* was also used as a requisitioned liner; allowing Orient Line to maintain the mail service while the government had control over berth allocations in her passenger areas.

In April, *Oronsay* was called up for use as a troop transport. She was hastily refurbished to add over 1,100 additional berths, almost doubling her capacity.

Orion was removed from trooping duties in April, instead deployed in Norway as a depot ship to support

Oronsay 1925–42 20,001grt. *Oronsay's* officers survey the damage to the ship's chart room after it was destroyed by the Luftwaffe whilst taking part in the evacuation of troops from Saint-Nazaire in France. In a remarkable feat of navigation, her captain brought his damaged ship back to England with nothing more than a schoolboy's atlas and ruler. (Henderson/Cremer Collection, ref. 10480)

Did You Know?

The *Narvik* was a Liberty-class ship.

the Allied landings in that region. The Allies would ultimately lose the Norwegian Campaign in June 1940, but before the defeat *Orion* returned to trooping duties.

On 9 May, while sailing off Dover, *Orontes* was attacked from the air by German bombers. Fortunately the bombing run caused no damage to the ship and she was able to make a subsequent voyage to Australia. She carried Australian troops to Singapore along with a consignment of Australian built Wirraway and Hudson Aircraft.

As the situation in Europe worsened, Orient's fleet bore witness to the great evacuations of the Continent. In May the London-bound *Ormonde* passed the massive Dunkirk evacuation fleet, while *Oronsay* and *Orama* were sent north to assist with the evacuation of Norway. *Ormonde* spent June 1940 assisting with the evacuation of Europe. That same month *Orama*, having been ordered to make her way back to Great Britain, was confronted by the German cruiser *Admiral Hipper* and destroyer *Hanz Lody*.

Orama had no chance of escape and was overcome by the German ships' firepower. She was lost with heavy casualties. German ships picked up 279 survivors, many of whom would spend the remainder of the war in prisoner of war camps, although a small group were released in 1943.

Cunard R.M.S. Lancastria   TONNAGE 16,500

Lancastria 1922–40 16,243 grt. *Lancastria* was sunk in June 1940 in France. *Oronsay* assisted in collecting the survivors of the disaster. (Ian Boyle, Simplon Postcards)

Otranto II 1926–57 20,032grt. *Otranto,* as an assault landing craft ship in World War II participated in the invasion of North Africa and Sicily. This photograph shows her landing craft and defensive ordinance. (Henderson/Cremer Collection, ref. OH8527)

Georgic 1932–55 27,759 grt. *Georgic*, the last ship built for the White Star Line, was bombed in Port Tewfik, Suez, in 1941. This heightened tensions and encouraged shipping lines to avoid land during the night hours. (George Frame Collection)

Oronsay was sent to assist with the evacuation of France on 17 June 1940. She was deployed to the French shipbuilding port of Saint-Nazaire. During the evacuation efforts she was attacked, sustaining damage to her bridge and resulting in a loss of the chart room and any direct communication with her engine room. Remarkably the ship's company were able to regain control of the vessel.

Nearby, on that same day, the Cunard vessel *Lancastria* was bombed and sunk. *Lancastria* was carrying thousands of people, well in excess of her design limits, as she and other ships attempted to hurriedly evacuate people from France. It is unclear exactly how many people were aboard the ship at the time of the attack, but it is generally believed that as many as 4,000 people were lost.

Oronsay was nearby and she assisted in collecting survivors from the disaster, taking those she rescued back to Britain for repatriation and medical attention.

In August, *Ormonde* was briefly taken off the evacuation service and loaded with 2,500 troops bound for Suez. Once in Suez she was ordered to India and South Africa to collect food before returning to Great Britain to re-join the evacuation fleet.

Having survived being bombed during the Norwegian evacuations, the *Oronsay* was given temporary repairs to her damaged bridge before being pressed back into service as part of the Children Overseas Reception Scheme.

In this role, she embarked over 300 children on 10 August and sailed for Halifax, Canada.

Upon her return, *Oronsay* was allocated to a convoy bound for Egypt. On 8 October, the convoy was attacked with *Oronsay* suffering significant damage to her engines, as well as both casualties and severe injuries among her troops.

Due to the danger posed by enemy shipping and aircraft, the convoy proceeded without *Oronsay*, however her engineers worked diligently and were able to reactivate the ship's engines, allowing her to return to Great Britain where she was refurbished in Glasgow before returning to service.

In 1941 the Orient Line's fleet was operating a variety of duties for the Admiralty in support of the war effort. Many ships were lost or damaged during their wartime service, including the Cunard-White Star Line's *Georgic*, which was bombed in the Gulf of Suez, Egypt.

Ships had already been ordered to stay away from land during night-time hours, and the July 1941 attack on *Georgic* only heightened an already tense situation. This was no more closely felt than aboard the refurbished and repaired *Oronsay*, which was in nearby waters at the time of the *Georgic* bombing.

Later that year, in September, the *Orion,* in convoy, collided with the

Orford 1928–40 19,941grt. A fine view of *Orford* in Sydney Harbour. Requisitioned in World War II as a transport, *Orford* was assisting in the movement of Free French troops when she was bombed in June 1940 by the Luftwaffe in Marseilles. Burnt out and beached, she was finally broken up in 1947. (Henderson/Cremer Collection, ref. 10718)

Oronsay 1925–42 20,001grt. A final look at *Oronsay* in Sydney Harbour proudly flying the Royal Mail pennant. Serving as a World War II troop transport, *Oronsay* was lost in the Atlantic Ocean to the Italian submarine *Archimede* on 9 October 1942. (Henderson/ Cremer Collection, ref. 10478)

Royal Navy's HMS *Revenge*, which unexpectedly swung into the path of the Orient liner. The ensuing collision caused significant damage to *Orion*'s bow. A faulty steering gear aboard *Revenge* combined with her duty officer ordering 'full astern' was blamed for the accident.

Remarkably, after makeshift repairs were completed, *Orion* was able to make way to Suez and disembarked her troops. She then proceeded to sail to Singapore, where she was given a comprehensive overhaul and her bow damage was repaired.

Later that October, *Orcades* was sent to Liverpool to collect troops bound for North Africa. However, once clearing the River Mersey the ship sailed for Halifax, where the troops were left with the US Navy for onward passage to Singapore.

As Japanese forces advanced throughout the Pacific arena, evacuations of troops and civilians took place with the help of Allied ships including the *Orion*, which was used in late December 1941 to evacuate injured troops and civilians from Kuala Lumpur. She sailed for Fremantle, Australia, where the injured were landed and treated in local hospitals.

As 1941 drew to an end the Orient Line's Fenchurch Avenue headquarters in London was destroyed in a German

Orontes II 1929–62 19,970grt. While the dark clouds of war are gathering in Europe Orontes lies peacefully at anchor in Rabaul harbour on a cruise from Sydney in July 1939. (Henderson/Cremer Collection, ref. 10740)

Empire Orwell 1936–87 18,036grt. Formerly the German East Africa Lines' Pretoria. Taken over by the British in 1945 and refitted for service as a troopship. Management was given to the Orient Line, which was the only occasion that the line managed a British troopship in peacetime. Orient Line management ceased in 1957. (Henderson/Cremer Collection, ref. 10313)

air raid. As a result, Orient Line's staff had to find new accommodation. Fortunately key shareholder P&O were able to accommodate them.

On 15 February 1942 the Japanese captured Singapore, making the waters in the region increasingly more dangerous for Allied shipping. At the time of the Singaporean invasion, Orcades was en route to Singapore with the I Corps of the Australian Army, however the ship was diverted to Sumatra before being ordered to nearby Batavia (Jakarta), where the troops were landed.

By this stage of the conflict, many ocean liners from a variety of operators were under the control of the Ministry of Shipping to perform non-trooping duties during World War II.

With Orient Line's fleet increasingly involved in Admiralty requisitions, the Ministry of Shipping engaged the company's passenger and cargo transport expertise to manage four Dutch vessels of the Nederland Royal Mail Line.

Christiaan Huygens, *Johan van Oldenbarneveldt*, *Johan de Witt* and *Marnix van St Aldegonde* all came under the Orient banner during the war, sailing on a variety of voyages including troopship duties. Despite being under Orient management, they retained their Dutch crew during their wartime service.

The Line also managed the cargo-carrying Liberty Ships *Samkansa* and *Sameveron*. At just over 7,000 tons, 137.5m in length, and with a top speed of 11.5 knots, the Liberty Ships were generally characterised as slow, ugly and ungainly, yet they were critical to the war effort.

An unprecedented 2,710 ships in this class were built. This was achieved by eighteen shipyards across the United States, which devised a method where prefabricated sections were welded together, allowing the ships to be completed in just a fraction of the time it would normally take to construct a vessel of this type.

The sheer numbers and speed at which these ships could be produced meant that the Allies had a transport that could be replaced quickly to counter the losses from the Kriegsmarine. This ability gave the Allies a significant advantage.

With so many Liberty Ships built, some were under the purview of the British Admiralty, including *Samkansa* and *Sameveron*.

In 1942 *Ormonde* was reconfigured to increase her trooping numbers. Having initially had her on-board accommodation restricted due to concerns over the ship's galley capabilities, the vessel was refurbished, increasing her capacity to over 3,500. This included the installation of more than 2,300 hammocks.

In May the Allies commenced an invasion of Madagascar with the aim of taking the island from the Vichy French Government, thus securing the region against possible Japanese use. *Oronsay* was used to transport Allied troops and stores to the island in support of this action, with the Allies claiming victory in November.

The Blue Funnel Liner *Tuscan Star* was sunk on 6 September 1942 by German submarine *U-109*. She had sailed from Buenos Aires and Santos bound for Liverpool and was carrying the British Consul General of Brazil, who escaped in a lifeboat along with the ship's captain, chief engineer and a number of women and children. *Otranto* picked up the lifeboat and brought the survivors aboard where they were fed and clothed.

Oronsay was lost on 9 October while heading north from Cape Town. The ship was hit by multiple torpedoes fired from the Italian submarine *Archimede*. The resulting damage caused explosions in the boiler and engine rooms, disabling the ship, and causing unmanageable flooding.

The ship was evacuated and just under three hours after she was first

Did You Know?

Captain Zawada of *Narvik*, which rescued the crew of *Orcades*, was decorated for his bravery and later emigrated to Australia on an Orient Line ship.

attacked a third torpedo hit *Oronsay*, causing her to sink. Due to the time between the initial and final torpedo strikes, it is widely believed the captain of *Archimede* allowed those aboard *Oronsay* to escape.

That same day, *Orcades* was also en-route to Great Britain from Cape Town when she passed wreckage and floating debris from a previously lost Allied ship. The atmosphere aboard *Orcades* was already tense, owing to her passenger complement of wounded soldiers, women and children. To help protect against potential attack, the ship's master, Captain Fox, ordered all passengers and crew to carry their life jackets with them as the ship steamed north.

The following day, on 10 October, U-172 spotted *Orcades* and fired a torpedo into the Orient Liner's port side. The damage caused the propeller and steering gear to malfunction. Captain Fox ordered abandon ship, but in the ensuing chaos one boat overturned, killing the occupants aboard.

Captain Fox and a fifty-one-man crew remained aboard the stricken ship in an attempt to either beach her or return her to Cape Town. The ship made way at a slow 6 knots for the next five hours until a further three torpedoes hit the liner, causing her to sink.

The 1,040 surviving members of the *Orcades* were picked up by the Polish vessel *Narvik*, which later collected Captain Fox and the rest of *Orcades*' surviving crew, before returning under escort to Cape Town.

On 17 October the Royal Navy brought welcome news when 266 survivors of the *Oronsay* sinking were picked up. However, one of the boats that escaped the ship had become separated from the rest and was later collected by the Vichy French naval vessel *Dumont d'Urville* and this took them to Dakar, Senegal, where they were held as prisoners of war.

On 8 November 1942 the Allies commenced Operation Torch, which was a British and United States effort to capture North Africa. *Ormonde*, *Orion* and *Otranto* were utilised for their trooping capacity, with *Orion* moving over 5,300 people to Algiers. The following month, *Orontes* joined her fleet mates in service in North Africa.

The 22 January 1943 annual general meeting was shrouded in the same secrecy that had enveloped the Orient Line management throughout the war. The managers were unable to discuss in any detail much of the wartime services due to the classified nature of the maritime war operations. The managers issued the following statement:

> For security reasons, we regret being unable to give you the information we should like to have given regarding your ships; but this can be said, throughout the year under review they have been under requisition and fully and gallantly employed on Government service ... All cash available for investment has been used in the purchase of Government War Loans.

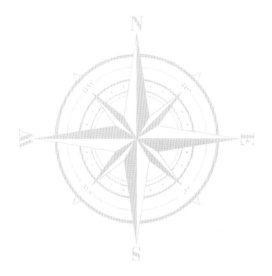

Did You Know?

In 1945, following the end of hostilities, the Deutsche Ost-Afrika Linie ship, *Pretoria*, was handed over to the British. They renamed her *Empire Doon* and she performed trooping duties under the management of Orient Line. In 1948 she was given a major refurbishment as a result of engine problems and was renamed *Empire Orwell*. She continued to perform military transportation duties under Orient Line management until 1957, when she was returned to the Ministry of Transport.

As the Allied war effort concentrated on capturing Axis occupied land, the Orient Line fleet was moved into support roles throughout the Mediterranean. To this end, on 29 June *Ormonde* sailed from Scotland bound for Sicily, where her troops were offloaded in Augusta. Following this, she was then ordered to the Pacific arena, stopping at Bombay (Mumbai), India to collect troops destined to join the British Fourteenth Army in Burma (Myanmar).

Otranto was also called on in the Mediterranean, having been converted into an assault ship, this time under the remit of the US Military in support of the first Allied mainland advance on Italy. During the July operation *Otranto* was attacked by a German bomber, however fortunately the bombs missed the ship and she was able to escape major damage.

In September 1943 *Orion* was employed on transatlantic trooping duties, carrying American servicemen from New York to Great Britain. During these voyages, the 1,400-berth liner was modified to carry upwards of 7,000 troops. Special consideration had to be made aboard for the movement of the personnel to ensure the stability of the ship was maintained. As such, a strict schedule was in place for the duration of the voyages.

From late 1944 until the end of the war, the Orient fleet were occupied in support of the steadily advancing Allied forces across Europe. This activity involved the fleet operating throughout the Mediterranean including Sicily, Malta and Egypt, while also being utilised in support of the Allied efforts in the Pacific.

Germany surrendered on 8 May 1945, signalling an end of the conflict in Europe. In June, *Orontes* returned to Australia for the first time in five years. It was the first visit of an Orient Line ship since *Orcades* in 1942.

When Japan surrendered on 15 August 1945, the fighting of World War II came to an end. The subsequent formal signing of the surrender aboard the USS *Missouri* on 2 September 1945 brought to a close the bloodiest war in the history of mankind.

Post-War
Rebuilding

10

Following the end of hostilities, Orient Line was once again left with only four ships in their fleet, all of which were still under government requisition. This left Orient Line dependent on the fees they received from the government for this service, as well as their investments. They were therefore keen to reinstate their Australian mail schedule and to rebuild their fleet for such a purpose.

On 17 September 1945 a new keel was laid down at Vickers-Armstrongs. The new ship, which was to be named *Orcades*, was to be built with a welded hull, meaning that the use of rivets was to be limited, with seams welded together to create a strong and watertight structure. The use of hull welding in shipbuilding was a relatively new technique in Britain and offered many benefits, including weight savings, speed, strength and the ease of joining curved shapes.

The Orient fleet continued in government service for the whole of 1945. Even after the war officially ended the Orient liners continued to be used as troop transports, repatriating soldiers and their families. In October *Orion* returned prisoners of war from Hong Kong to Britain. The next month she was in the headlines when Australian officers walked off the ship, which was due to take them home, in protest at the accommodation provided to them aboard. They were upset that they were to be housed in tiered berths rather than cabins. On 13 November, only two days after she left port, *Orion* was back, suffering engine problems.

In January the following year *Otranto* was used to repatriate British troops from India. In March there was a smallpox outbreak on *Orontes* and she was quarantined at Southampton.

Orion's war duties ended in early April 1946, and she was sent for refit at Vickers-Armstrongs. Reconditioning took longer than expected and it wasn't until the following year that she was ready to recommence the Orient Line mail service.

Ormonde completed her war duties in October 1946 and was sent for reconditioning in Birkenhead. As she was now an older ship, having entered service in 1917, she was no longer suitable for the mail service. Instead, she was to be refitted to carry emigrants to Australia under the assisted passage scheme. Her passenger accommodation was altered to offer a single 'austerity' class with a maximum capacity of 1,050.

On 12 February 1947 *Otranto*, which continued in government service, had a collision with a cargo ship, *Samrich*, but fortunately sustained only minor damage. On 25 February *Orion* left on the first post-war sailing for Orient's Australian mail service. She was the first of the Orient Liners to return to merchant service and it was a great relief for Orient to finally have a steamer back under their control.

In April 1947 *Orontes* was released by the Ministry of Transport. She was

Otranto II 1926–57 20,032grt. A formidable post-World War II image of *Otranto*. During her war service the *Otranto* carried some 150,000 personnel and travelled over 330,000 miles. (Henderson/Cremer Collection, ref. OH6228)

to be reconditioned in Southampton by Messrs. J.I. Thorneycroft & Co.

By October 1947 work on *Ormonde* was completed and on 10 October she departed on her first voyage to Australia as an emigrant ship. She was run on this service in conjunction with a number of P&O liners, including *Ranchi* and *Chitral*, as well as older ships from some of the other British lines, including Cunard. The assisted passage scheme was designed to boost the population of Australia by offering very favourable conditions for British citizens willing to relocate there.

The passengers were chosen by the Australian Government, with ex-servicemen and their families offered free passage, and civilians offered passage for the nominal sum of £10, leading to these emigrants becoming known as 'ten-pound poms'. The assisted passage scheme was eventually extended to include people wishing to migrate from various other countries, including the United States and Belgium, but these emigrants were not offered anywhere near as much assistance by the Australian Government.

Ormonde's first sailing under the Australian Government Scheme of Migration was fully booked with people who had been selected to sail by the Australian Government. The voyage did

Orcades III 1948–73 28,164grt. Lady Morshead, wife of the Orient Lines' Australian general manager, inspects the hull of *Orcades* before she steps up to the dais and launches the largest ship then built for the line on 14 October 1947. (Henderson/Cremer Collection, ref. 10406)

Orcades III 1948–73 28,164grt. Riding easily in her natural element, *Orcades* was built by Vickers-Armstrongs Ltd at their Barrow-in-Furness yards. (Henderson/Cremer Collection, ref. 10410)

Orcades III 1948–73 28,164grt. A photograph taken during her trials off Arran, showing her original funnel before she was equiped with a 'Welsh Hat' designed to avoid distributing smuts over the after decks. (Henderson/Cremer Collection, ref. OH6204)

Orient Line ships sailing to or from Australia to London would call at Naples, where mails were transferred to the Orient Line Express train for quick despatch to London, reaching there a week before the ship. Passengers also made use of the special train, often to avoid the Bay of Biscay. The Orient Line Express was started in 1903 by the Italian authorities to expedite the British mail service across Europe. (Henderson/Cremer Collection, ref. OH6043)

not provide the same level of comfort that was experienced aboard *Ormonde* prior to the war, and not to the standard of the Orient Line generally, with the ship having limited furniture and an increased passenger capacity from her days of sailing as a single-tourist-class ship.

Four days after *Ormonde* left on her new service, Orient Line celebrated the launch of *Orcades*. She was launched on 14 October 1947 by Lady Morshead, wife of the Sydney manager of the Orient Line, Sir James Morshead. *Orcades* had a single funnel and single mast that was incorporated in the one central structure. She had a far more modern profile than the earlier Orient ships, with her bridge placed amidships. The funnel had no cowl ventilators and she was powered by Parsons double-reduction geared turbines, which drove two screws.

On the same day that they launched *Orcades*, Orient Line announced that they had placed an order for another new vessel, this one to be named *Oronsay*. The new ship was again to be built at Vickers-Armstrongs.

During 1948 the shares of Anderson, Green & Co. Ltd, which managed Orient Line, were acquired by Orient

Oronsay II 1951–75 27,632grt. The sculpting of *Oronsay*'s single mast in the workshop at Vickers-Armstrongs, Barrow-in-Furness. Following the example set with *Orcades III*, the *Oronsay* had a combined mast, funnel and bridge structure. (Henderson/Cremer Collection, ref. 10482)

Oronsay II 1951–75 27,632grt. Launched on 30 June 1950, the *Oronsay II* was very nearly lost when she caught fire in the fitting-out dock but was saved by a massive effort by firemen from Barrow and surrounding towns. (Henderson/Cremer Collection, ref. 10485)

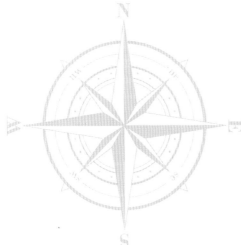

Steam Navigation Company Ltd. This effectively merged the holdings of Anderson, Green & Co. Ltd, which included more than just the Orient Line management, with the Orient Line. Practically, there was very little change at the Orient Line, as the directors of Anderson, Green & Co. had been the de facto directors of Orient Line prior to the purchase of their shares and were now the directors of Orient Line proper. This change was required due to the new Companies Act 1947, which stated that all limited companies needed to have a board of directors.

In May 1948 *Orontes*, having been reconditioned, was released from requisition. She sailed on her first post-war voyage to Australia on 17 June. *Otranto* remained in government service, being sent to Cammell Laird and Co. of Liverpool for reconversion to a merchant ship in the second half of 1948. During her military career *Otranto* had steamed 335,655 miles, and carried 132,191 troops, 3,181 civilians and 10,076 prisoners of war.

Orcades left England on her maiden voyage to Australia on 14 December. She was under the command of Captain Charles Fox and carried twenty-three officers and crew members who had all served on the previous *Orcades*. She also carried the chronometer of her forbear.

Oronsay II 1951–75 27,632grt. *Oronsay* as originally built with her controversial upright funnel. She was later fitted with a 'Welsh Hat' to effectively disperse soot from falling on the decks. (Henderson/Cremer Collection, ref. OH6215)

Oronsay II 1951–75 27,632grt. *Oronsay* being led to her Pyrmont berth in Sydney Harbour. In 1954 *Oronsay* pioneered the Pacific route for the Line with a sailing from Sydney to North America and back. (Henderson/Cremer Collection, ref. 10690)

Oronsay II 1951–75 27,632grt. During her Orient Line service from 1951–60 the *Oronsay* made twenty-seven Australian line voyages and carried 37,460 passengers. Including her P&O years, she made a total of sixty-four line voyages and carried some 76,000 passengers. (Henderson/Cremer Collection, ref. 10486)

Oronsay II 1951–75 27,632grt. An Orient Line-issued postcard of *Oronsay* in Orient colours of corn-coloured hull with green boot-topping. (Henderson/Cremer Collection, ref. 10492)

Orcades made her maiden arrival in Sydney on 14 January 1949. Her voyage from London to Fremantle took twenty-two days, fifty minutes, and was a record, with a service speed of 22.75 knots.

Early in 1949 *Oronsay* was laid down at Vickers-Armstrongs. *Oronsay* was to be built to a similar design to *Orcades* and was built on the same slipway.

In June 1949 the last of the Orient Liners under requisition was finally returned to the Line. *Otranto* left for her first voyage to Australia as a one-class tourist ship on 14 July. Her schedule to Fremantle was twenty-six days and she continued in this service until 1957, except for a single voyage in 1950.

In early 1950 a Welsh Hat was added to the top of *Orcades*' funnel in an attempt to resolve the soot and smoke issues. The Welsh Hat was, as the name suggests, a hat-shaped cap that was fitted to the top of the funnel to concentrate and direct the soot from the engines up and away from the decks. It was a very distinctive-looking device that did indeed look like a Welsh Hat or top hat, hence its nicknames.

In May 1950 *Ormonde* was chartered by the Dutch Government for a number of voyages to evacuate their nationals from Jakarta and in August *Otranto* was similarly employed. This was a result of the formation of Indonesia from what had been the Dutch East Indies.

On 30 June that same year *Oronsay* was launched at Barrow-in-Furness. She was christened by Mrs A.I. Anderson, wife of the chairman. *Oronsay* was the twenty-second passenger ship to be built for the Orient Steam Navigation Co.

Oronsay was moved to the Buccleuch Dock for fitting out, with the expectation she would be completed in time to enter service in early 1951. Unfortunately, fitting out was to take considerably longer than expected because on 28 October flames were seen coming from the No. 2 hold. The fire was in the insulating cork and had been smouldering for hours before it was noticed. Multiple fire brigades responded to the emergency, assisting the shipyard in fighting the fire.

It took all night to get the fire under control and in the interim more damage had occurred. *Oronsay* had developed a heavy list towards the dock during the night due to the water being poured into her. Holes were cut into the side of the ship, attempting to reduce the level of water and by extension the scale of the list. Later, as the list increased these holes had to be plugged to stop more water from pouring in.

With the ship a smoking mess it was decided to postpone *Oronsay*'s maiden voyage and a new date was set for 16 May 1951. When the ship was inspected on 1 November it was discovered that the damage was not as bad as had first been thought and the fitting out was able to continue.

The work was completed on 15 May 1951, one day before she was due to sail on her maiden voyage. The maiden voyage nonetheless departed on schedule, with the ship first seeing Australian shores on 8 June.

Did You Know?

There were some famous Australian cricketers present at the launch of *Orsova II*, including Richie Benaud.

Oronsay II 1951–75 27,632grt. The liner, in P&O colours, passes under the Golden Gate Bridge in San Francisco, repeating her pioneering Pacific voyage of 1954 when she opened the new Orient Line service across the Pacific. (Henderson/Cremer Collection, ref. OH6048)

Oronsay II 1951–75 27,632grt. Resplendent in P&O colours, *Oronsay* makes a striking sight as she sails down Sydney Harbour. (Henderson/Cremer Collection, ref. OH6217)

A panoramic view of Pyrmont/Jones Bay wharves, Sydney, on 15 November 1955, with three Orient liners alongside: *Orcades III*, *Oronsay II* and *Otranto II*. (Henderson/ Cremer Collection, ref. 10382)

In October *Oronsay* was used to evacuate wives and children of British servicemen from Port Said. There had been increased tensions in Suez and the British Government decided to bring sixty-one women and one hundred and six children to Britain in case of conflict.

In early 1952 another liner was laid down at Vickers-Armstrongs. The *Orsova* was to be a ship of 210.61m length and 27.61m beam. She was given the yard number 1021 and was to be built using prefabricated sections.

During the English summer *Oronsay* made her first cruise from Tilbury to the Mediterranean. The voyage lasted thirteen days and was a success.

Later that year it was time for *Ormonde* to finally leave the fleet. She made her final voyage to Australia, flying a 210ft paying off pennant. She arrived back in Tilbury on 19 November 1952. She was then sold to the British Iron and Steel Corporation to be broken up.

In May the following year *Orsova* was launched by Lady Anderson, wife of Sir Colin Anderson, chairman of Orient Line. Just two hours later P&O launched their latest liner, *Arcadia*, on the Clyde.

Orsova had a similar design to the previous two Orient Line ships, but with some key differences. She had no mast and her funnel carried the wireless aerials and halyards. She was built with a Welsh Hat, for dispersing smoke and was fitted with 8,873m^3 of refrigerated space. She was also the first British passenger liner built using an all-welded

Did You Know?

During the new *Orsova*'s maiden visit to Melbourne on 16 April 1955 Orsova Nina Wilson Ingram Staunton Hodgson, by then Mrs Lynott, was a guest of Captain Whinfield aboard her new namesake.

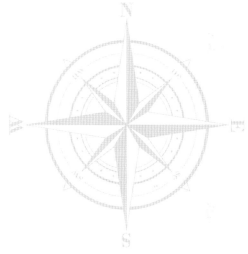

Opposite: Another panoramic view taken on 15 November 1955 showing from left *Orontes II, Oronsay II* and *Orcades III*. A wonderful image with the Sydney Harbour Bridge and the row of wharves, opposite the ships, which have since been reclaimed and redeveloped into the Barangaroo precinct of Sydney. (Henderson/Cremer Collection, ref. 10383)

Orsova II 1954–74 28,790grt. *Orsova* differed from her sisters *Orcades* and *Oronsay* in that she was given a dramatically flared bow, the forepeak is shown here being lowered into position. (Henderson/Cremer Collection, ref. 10545)

Orsova II 1954–74 28,790grt. *Orsova* in profile at speed. The liner was built without a traditional mast. (Henderson/Cremer Collection, ref. P&O_339)

Orsova II 1954–74 28,790grt. *Orsova* was a beautiful ship that had her career cut short owing to economic circumstances. (Henderson/Cremer Collection, ref. OH6117)

Orsova II 1954–74 28,790grt. *Orsova* in P&O colours at Sydney. (Henderson/Cremer Collection, ref. P&O_338)

Orsova II 1954–74 28,790grt. An *Orsova* postcard showing her in original Orient Line livery. (Henderson/Cremer Collection, ref. 10550)

the panama way

by

ORIENT LINE

USA CANADA AUSTRALIA

design. She had a distinctive swan neck bow, which set her apart from the rest of the fleet.

In June 1953 *Orcades* took part in the Coronation Naval Review for Queen Elizabeth II off Spithead. Under command of Captain (later Commodore) Whinfield, she carried government guests and led the merchant vessels through the lines of assembled ships.

In the new year *Oronsay* commenced transpacific voyages for Orient Line. She departed Sydney on 1 January, stopping at Auckland, Suva, Honolulu, Victoria, Vancouver and San Francisco, returning by the same ports. The round trip lasted thirty-nine days. The transpacific route had been left open the previous June when Canadian Australasian Line had withdrawn their ship *Aorangi* from the service.

The voyage to San Francisco proved popular and five transpacific voyages were made during the year, three by *Oronsay*, and one each by *Orion* and *Orcades*.

Orsova departed on 17 March on her maiden voyage to Australia with workmen still on board completing the

fit out of the first-class verandah bar. To apologise for the inconvenience, Orient offered first-class guests a 10 per cent refund on their passage, but as the work was completed during the journey, a number of passengers refused to take the refund.

Orsova made her first Pacific voyage on 28 January 1955. She broke a speed record for merchant ships, sailing between San Francisco and Honolulu in three days, seventeen hours.

The following year *Orsova* ran aground in Port Philip Bay, but was refloated with no major damage. The Port of Melbourne Marine Board had recently made the decision to amalgamate the river pilots and sea pilots and as a result the river pilots, who had considerably less experience with vessels the size and speed of *Orsova*, were sometimes called upon to pilot them. This was the case with *Orsova*, with the enquiry finding that though the pilot was at fault for the grounding it was 'unfortunate' that he had been given the task in the first place as he did not have the requisite experience for a liner of that size.

A 1959 Orient Line-issued brochure promoting 'the panama way' with a none too subtle show of the hands and moustache indicating round the world voyages, a route pioneered by Orient Lines' *Orsova* in 1955. (Henderson/Cremer Collection, ref. folio8_01954)

11

P&O – Orient Line

The August 1955 return passage of *Orontes* to Britain, from Australia, was diverted via Cape Town at the request of the British Admiralty. The following month *Oronsay* was also routed via Cape Town. With escalating tensions over the Suez Canal it was no longer deemed safe to travel via that route. The Suez Crisis closed the Canal to merchant shipping from October 1956 to March 1957. This, of course, resulted in a significantly longer journey for the Orient Line ships.

Otranto ended her Orient Line career in May 1957. She arrived in London at the end of her final emigrant passenger service on 13 May and was sold for breaking up at the British Iron and Steel Corporation.

Later that year *Orcades* was involved in a collision whilst in Aden. In August, while manoeuvring with the aid of tugs, *Orcades* collided with the French vessel *Picardie*. She was blown off course and crashed due to high winds at the time.

Later during that same voyage she was caught in a severe monsoon. The heat on board caused the death of two passengers from heat exhaustion.

On 18 September 1957 the keel was laid for what was to be the final Orient Line passenger ship. *Oriana* was given the yard number 1061 at Vickers-Armstrongs. The name was derived from Gloriana, the name given by contemporary poets to Queen Elizabeth I.

Oriana 1960–86 41,915grt. A greyhound of the seas in every sense, *Oriana*'s unusual and dramatic profile is shown in this wonderful early photograph. (Henderson/Cremer Collection, ref. 11299)

Oriana 1960–86 41,915grt. It is 9 December 1960 and *Oriana* rides at anchor at Port Said on her maiden voyage to Australia. (Henderson/Cremer Collection, ref. P&O_380)

Did You Know?

Oriana's badge design was two 'E's, surrounded by an Ω. The badge was designed to symbolise the link between the two Elizabethan ages.

In December *Orcades* went to the aid of a sick sailor on the *Glenmoor*, a British cargo vessel. The rescue was performed in very heavy seas and he was taken aboard *Orcades* to Fremantle, where the ship arrived on Boxing Day.

The following year on 22 October a fire broke out in the hospital aboard *Oronsay*. The ship's surgeons were woken in the early hours by a burning smell and discovered thick smoke in the hospital. The fire had been inadvertently started by a sick passenger, who had left clothing on a heater. The fire was extinguished without too much damage.

The year 1958 was to bring more changes to the Orient Line service. They were now facing more competition than ever. Not only were they still competing with the other shipping lines, but jet aircraft were beginning to become a major threat to the industry.

The first commercial flight of a Boeing 707 occurred on 26 October 1958 and it meant big changes for all the shipping companies. The airliner was the first successful commercial jet aircraft and within a matter of years it totally revolutionised the way that people travelled. No longer were passengers bound to take month-long sea voyages to cross the world; now they could fly.

Unlike many other shipping companies, Orient Line seems to have been aware of the potential for aircraft to rival shipping from quite early on. It was written in a statement to the shareholders regarding the annual general meeting on 22 January 1943 that:

> It will be remembered that in 1936 you authorised the Company to take power to invest in or operate air transport, and we made investments accordingly … travel by air will be a great and increasing factor in world transport.

Oriana 1960–86 41,915grt. With an escort of tugs and small craft, *Oriana* makes her triumphal maiden arrival at Sydney on 30 December 1960. (Henderson/Cremer Collection, ref. OH6034)

Although Orient Line did not end up operating any transport aircraft, they did make adjustments to their services. They refitted their ships, with *Orion* changing to a two-class tourist layout in 1958, offering both cabin and tourist class. They increased their cruising itineraries and began to offer formal entertainment on board.

The offering of entertainment on board was a big change for ships in the late 1950s and early 1960s, and meant that ships started to have staff dedicated to this role. Prior to this passengers had organised their own entertainments, usually with some assistance from the officers and crew.

To improve the fleet's cruising capabilities, in 1959 *Orcades* and *Oronsay* were both refurbished and fitted with air conditioning. *Orcades* was given her cruising refit at Harland and Wolff in January, with the works taking ten weeks. In addition to adding air conditioning, the decks were renamed, with the upper decks given the names Sun Deck, Stadium Deck and Verandah Deck. The interior spaces were updated, with a new swimming pool and restaurants replacing the dining halls.

Oronsay's refit was very similar, taking place in September at Gladstone Dock in Liverpool. Works on *Oronsay* were delayed by industrial issues, with six stoppages during the refit. As a result of this Orient never sent work to Liverpool again.

On 3 November *Oriana* was launched by Princess Alexandra. *Oriana* had an aluminium superstructure, which gave great weight savings and allowed for a taller superstructure than would have been possible if steel had been used for her whole construction. To improve her speed, fuel efficiency and reduce drag, *Oriana* was given a bulbous bow. She was fitted with double-reduction geared turbines of Pametreda design. She had two sets of machinery each with high and medium turbines. This gave *Oriana* a service speed of 27.5 knots.

Orsova was given her cruising refurbishment at Vickers-Armstrongs in early 1960. Like her sister ships, her decks were renamed. Additionally, her first-class restaurant became the ship's grillroom and her two saloons were recreated as restaurants. To make *Orsova* more comfortable in the tropics the air conditioning was extended throughout the ship.

Whilst she was in refit, the P&O and Orient Line fleets were merged. The joint venture became known as P&O Orient Line. With increasing competition from the jet causing greater pressure on the shipping companies, it was reasoned that merging the two would reduce running costs by reducing the need to duplicate shore-side services.

Meanwhile, fitting out of *Oriana* was progressing well at the Vickers-Armstrongs yard. On 21 October HM The Queen and HRH The Duke of Edinburgh, together with Lord Mountbatten, toured the *Oriana*. They had been at the yard for the launch of the HMS *Dreadnought*.

Oriana proceeded to sea trials, during which time she was subject to rough weather, which caused damage to the

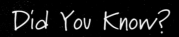

SS *United States* and RMS *Queen Mary* were in port the day *Oriana* departed on her maiden voyage to Australia.

glass sliding bookcase doors in the library, broke hinges on doors elsewhere on the ship and sent a grand piano flying down the stairs to its demise. Despite the damage, *Oriana* proved herself, attaining 30.64 knots during her speed trials, which were held in a gale.

In November *Oriana* departed on a five-day shakedown cruise to Lisbon.

The following month *Oriana* was ready to begin her passenger service. On 2 December she was visited by Princess Alexandra and the Duchess of Kent. The following day she departed on her maiden voyage to Australia, arriving in Sydney on 30 December. She was the first ship to dock at the new Overseas Passenger Terminal, which

Oriana 1960–86 41,915grt. Barely room to move as *Oriana* transits the Panama Canal. (Henderson/Cremer Collection, ref. OH6118)

Oriana 1960–86 41,915grt. *Oriana* is edged alongside by a bevy of tugs at the partially built Sydney Overseas Passenger Terminal on her maiden arrival. This photograph shows the vast open deck areas. (Henderson/Cremer Collection, ref. OH6035)

Oriana 1960–86 41,915grt. Oriana alongside the passenger terminal at Sydney whilst the Orsova II passes under the Harbour Bridge after departing her Pyrmont berth on a voyage to England on 26 February 1961. (Henderson/Cremer Collection, ref. OH6040)

had been recently completed at a cost of £1.25 million.

From Australia Oriana continued on to San Francisco. The onward journey was supplemented by an agency of the Bank of New South Wales, which travelled aboard to offer banking facilities and currency exchange for the ship's passengers.

In 1961 P&O officially absorbed the Orient Line, purchasing the last of their shares. They created a new company, P&O-Orient Lines Ltd.

On 14 April 1961 Orontes anchored off Tobruk to mark the twentieth anniversary of the World War II siege. She carried on board twenty-three members of the Rats of Tobruk Association, survivors of the Australian Ninth Division.

In December of that year it was announced that Orontes was to be broken up. She was sold to J.F. Ordaz y Compania, Madrid, and departed the fleet in February 1962.

Orcades was transferred to P&O's books on 21 September 1962. Less than

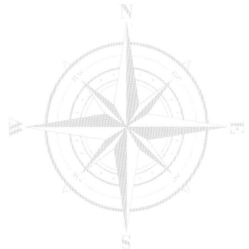

Above: *Orcades III* 1948–73 28,164grt. A fine view of *Orcades* in P&O white looming large in Sydney Harbour. (Henderson/Cremer Collection, ref. P&O_296)

Above right: *Oriana* 1960–86 41,915grt. *Oriana* lost none of her unique beauty in P&O colours, as seen in this wonderful aerial photograph. (Henderson/Cremer Collection, ref. P&O_340.207)

Opposite: *Orion* 1935–63 23,371grt. At the end of her life in 1963, *Orion* acted as a hotel ship alongside at Hamburg for the International Horticultural Exhibition – even after almost thirty years of service she still looked fresh and iconic. (Henderson/Cremer Collection, ref. P&O_378)

two months later it was announced that *Orion* was to be withdrawn from service eighteen months hence, but her career was not to last that long.

Oriana was involved in a collision with the US aircraft carrier USS *Kearsarge* in December of that year. The collision occurred near Long Beach in dense fog. The crash caused a 4.87m gash in *Oriana*'s bow and a fire in her paint storage area, but both ships were able to make their way to port without aid. *Oriana* was found to be at blame for the incident.

Orion was chartered from May to September of 1963 for use as a hotel ship in Hamburg during the International Horticulture Exhibition. At the end of her charter she was sold for scrap to Jos Boles & Son SA of Tamise, Belgium, where she arrived on 7 October at the end of a twenty-eight-year career.

The year 1964 brought a change to the appearance of the Orient liners, with all hull liveries being changed to P&O's white colour scheme. *Oronsay* was the first to be painted white in April of that year and at the same time she was transferred to P&O.

In that same year *Orcades* was reconfigured in a single tourist class. In her new configuration she could carry 1,635 passengers. A casino was added in what had once been the Tartan Bar. Her grill became a cinema and the original tourist-class lounge was replaced by a nightclub. These changes were intended to keep *Orcades* profitable in an increasingly difficult market.

The following year the last two remaining Orient Line-built vessels, *Oriana* and *Orsova*, were transferred to P&O registration.

12

The End of Orient

With the Orient Line ships gradually taking on a P&O identity throughout the 1960s it became less important to maintain the Orient name in the eyes of the company.

Orient was but a fraction of the size of P&O, which had an enviable reputation of its own, a reputation the line hoped would help it survive and remain relevant in the age of the jet.

The 1966 seamen's strike, which lasted from 16 May through to 1 July, significantly impacted all British shipping operators and P&O-Orient was no exception. The strike was an attempt to secure better wages and conditions but effectively crippled the nation, and all but destroyed the British passenger shipping industry, resulting in the Prime Minister of the United Kingdom declaring a state of emergency.

Orcades III 1948–73 28,164grt. *Orcades* joins her running mate *Oriana* at Auckland on 26 November 1966. (Henderson/Cremer Collection, ref. OH6184)

Orcades III 1948–73 28,164grt. *Orcades* off Cape Town in 1967. During her career the *Orcades* made thirty-five Australian line voyages and carried 45,400 passengers. (Henderson/Cremer Collection, ref. P&O_335)

Orcades III 1948–73 28,164grt. June 1970 and *Orcades* encounters
extreme seas off the South Coast of Western Australia, damaging
her steering gear and forcing her to return to Fremantle for repairs.
(Henderson/Cremer Collection, ref. OH6201)

Demands included a 17 per cent salary increase and a shorter working week, however shipping operators had recently finalised an agreement with the union for a 13 per cent pay rise and the new demands were a bridge too far for operators of a transportation method already under serious threat from the airliner and containerisation.

Unlike some of their contemporaries, P&O-Orient survived the crisis, however the financial damage was significant, leading to further consolidation of the organisation's operations.

By 1966, ownership of the Orient fleet had all been transferred to P&O, an action that saw the use of P&O livery and house flag on all passenger liners of the combined fleet.

Thus, it came as little surprise when in November 1966 P&O dropped the Orient name altogether. But the remaining ships retained their distinctly Orient Line profiles and names, and would continue to enjoy loyalty from the passengers who had enjoyed the Orient Line experience for decades.

Further disruption impacted the P&O fleet in June 1967 when the Six-Day War closed the Suez Canal. This again led to the lengthy rerouting of company ships via Cape Town, adding costs to an already stretched budget. The additional cost brought on by the closure of the canal led P&O to cancel line voyages to the Far East in 1969 and India in 1970.

On 17 July 1967 the *Oronsay* was approaching Hong Kong with 853 passengers bound for Yokohama, Japan. As the ship was making her way through the Taiwan Strait, a fire broke out aboard the ship. The captain alerted Hong Kong authorities but the crew were able to contain the blaze.

However on 18 July, shortly after docking in Hong Kong, a fire broke out in the ship's holds, causing the captain to request assistance from local authorities. A dozen fire engines were dispatched to the ship and were fortunately able to control the blaze, which caused damage to more than forty cabins.

In April 1968, *Oriana* was making a westbound transit of the Panama Canal when she made contact with the bank, damaging her starboard propeller and propeller shaft.

Unfortunately, the damage was severe with the tail shaft being bent and several blades being lost from her propeller. Makeshift repairs proved unsuccessful so the ship sailed slowly to Southampton, where permanent repairs were completed.

The 1970s had an inauspicious start for P&O with two former Orient liners plagued with troubles within the first two months of the decade.

The troubles started in January when *Oronsay* was held in quarantine in Vancouver, Canada, due to a typhoid outbreak aboard. The extended stay resulted in cancelled voyages and cost the line over £500,000!

Then, the following month while stopped at Sydney, two of *Orsova*'s crewmembers were accused of murder, resulting in them having to leave the ship to stand before the court. Although

Did You Know?

A P&O spokesperson said to the *Canberra Times* 15 March 1986 of *Oriana*'s retirement, 'The *Oriana* is like an old fancy car – nice to look at but too expensive to run these days.'

Orcades III 1948–73 28,164grt. Another view of *Orcades* battling heavy seas on her return to Fremantle. She had sailed as normal on 22 June 1970 for Adelaide but damage sustained in the rough conditions forced her back to Fremantle on 22 June. After repairs she sailed on 26 June for Melbourne, omitting Adelaide. (Henderson/Cremer Collection, ref. OH6203)

both incidents were not the fault of P&O, the line suffered reputational damage as a result – something they could ill afford in their cash-strapped state.

In June the *Orcades*' steering gear was badly damaged in rough seas off Western Australia. The ship's engineers worked tirelessly for five hours to restore control and eventually were able to return the ship to Fremantle for permanent repairs.

That same month, while in Southampton water, a serious fire broke out in *Oriana*'s boiler room. Plumes of black smoke poured out of the ship's superstructure just aft of the bridge and the ship subsequently lost all motive power.

Oriana's passengers and crew were mustered and preparations were made to abandon ship while the fire fighting teams worked to put out the blaze. Fortunately local fireboats arrived on the scene and the ship was saved, though badly damaged.

She was towed back to her berth, where some of her passengers transferred to the nearby *QE2*, while those passengers who wished to stay aboard were accommodated in the ship while repairs were under way in the boiler room and associated areas.

Remarkably, *Oriana* was ready to sail by 27 August. As she departed her berth she passed the *QE2*, which had just returned from New York. The Cunard flagship's captain sent a message of good luck to the master of *Oriana* and both ships exchanged lengthy whistle blasts.

In February 1972 the *Orsova* received a request for assistance from the US tugboat *Tecuseh*. An officer aboard the tug had developed a thrombosis in his leg and needed urgent medical intervention. As *Orsova*'s hospital was well equipped, the ship made a 150-mile deviation from her course at high speeds in order to render assistance.

The following month saw the *Orcades* make her final departure from Sydney. She was to be retired later that year as P&O further reduced its passenger ship fleet in response to the ongoing decline in demand due to the increased popularity of jet aircraft.

During this voyage, *Orcades* went to the aid of a sailor aboard the Norwegian ore carrier *Berge Istra*. The sailor was injured and was given medical treatment in *Orcades*' hospital. Due to the closure of the Suez Canal, the ship sailed via Durban, South Africa, where the sailor disembarked.

Upon returning to Southampton, *Orcades* set about cruising for her final months of P&O service. She was eventually decommissioned on 13 October 1972, but remained alongside for eight weeks before sailing to Taiwan, where she was scrapped in 1973.

Later that year, *Oronsay* was also assigned to full-time cruising. Operating as a single-class ship, she sailed with a tourist-class capacity of 1,400 passengers.

In November the *Orsova* made headlines when 300 passengers and crew came down with dysentery. P&O asked all crew to undergo a test in an attempt to identify the carrier of the

Oriana 1960–86 41,915grt. During the final years of her career the *Oriana* was a familiar sight at South Pacific Island ports during cruises from Sydney. In this photograph she comes alongside at the Fijian port of Suva under the watchful eyes of the Fijian constabulary. (Henderson/Cremer Collection, ref. OH6033)

Oriana 1960–86 41,915grt. *Oriana* shown departing the Sydney Passenger Terminal on one of her final cruises in early 1986. (Henderson/Cremer Collection, ref. OH11901)

disease, however over 200 crew refused and were subsequently paid off and left the ship.

On 26 November *Orsova* was given a refurbishment aimed at improving the cruising amenities aboard. However, when she returned to service a shortfall in crew numbers caused problems for the ship's next voyage, resulting in the passenger complement being reduced to only 650 passengers.

This left many unhappy travellers on the dockside, while those who did travel with the ship voiced concerns about the quality of the food and conditions aboard, leading to P&O offering a full refund to all passengers.

In the summer of 1973, P&O made the shock decision to retire their flagship *Canberra*. Built in 1962, *Canberra* was both larger and newer than any of the former Orient liners, however the reduction of passengers on line voyages coupled with *Canberra*'s disastrous introduction to the American cruise market led the company to believe she had no future.

At the same time, P&O announced that the *Orsova* would take over *Canberra*'s cruise schedule from 1974, however by August the company had reversed their decision, opting to retain *Canberra* and retire *Orsova*. This proved to be a wise move, as *Canberra* went on to become a highly successful and much loved cruise ship, operating cruises from Southampton until 1997.

For *Orsova* this meant a three-month farewell season that culminated on 23 November when the ship embarked her last cruise passengers. Upon her return to Southampton she was emptied and decommissioned before sailing on 14 December to the Nan Feng Steel Enterprise Co. in Kaohsiung, Taiwan, for scrapping.

The year 1974 brought further change for P&O when it acquired the American cruise line Princess Cruises. P&O invested heavily in Princess, building on the success it had enjoyed with the purpose-built P&O cruise ship *Spirit of London*.

To meet the new cruising demand, class barriers were removed from all P&O ships, including the *Oronsay* and *Oriana*. The line acquired the *Island Princess* and *Sea Venture* for Princess, the latter being renamed *Pacific Princess*, and partnered with television production companies to film the hit series *The Love Boat* aboard those ships.

It was clear that P&O's future now lay in cruising, and by 1975 *Oriana* was cruising all year round. The last of the Orient liners were based in Southampton for the northern summer, before following the sun to Sydney for the remainder of the year.

Oronsay's time ran out in 1975 with the veteran Orient liner now unable to compete with the new wave of dedicated cruise tonnage. Her final voyage was announced in April, a trip that saw her sail from Sydney to Hong Kong via Brisbane.

Oronsay arrived in Hong Kong at the end of that final cruise on

Oriana 1960–86 41,915grt. *Oriana*'s anchor chains being prepared to secure her to the wharf as she awaits her fate. (Henderson/Cremer Collection, ref. OH11902)

28 September and she was then de-stored and decommissioned. She made one final voyage to Taiwan, where she was scrapped.

With *Oronsay* out of service, *Oriana* remained the sole survivor of the Orient Line. Her cruising career saw her establish a number of itineraries in the South Pacific, some of which are still popular with the P&O Australia fleet today.

In May 1978 *Oriana* was undertaking a repositioning itinerary when P&O's Southampton office received a bomb threat. The British Government were notified, and sent out bomb disposal experts on a RAF C-130 to assist the liner.

By the time the aircraft approached *Oriana*, her security crew had already conducted a thorough search of the ship and nothing was found. As a result, the bomb disposal team returned to Great Britain and the ship continued on to the Caribbean.

In 1981 P&O announced that *Oriana* would leave Southampton to be based full time in Sydney. In anticipation of her forthcoming departure from Britain, Princess Alexandra, The Hon. Angus Ogilvy and their children toured the ship.

Oriana left Southampton on 12 November, arriving in Sydney where she was 'Australianised' for her new full-time cruising role. Changes included the creation of a quintessential Aussie pub in the space once occupied by her Midships Bar.

The ship spent several years in Australia, but was never able to fully capture the market in the same way that Sitmar's *Fairstar* had done. A much smaller ship than *Oriana*, *Fairstar* was aggressively marketed as 'The Fun Ship' and became so well known that the name *Fairstar* practically became the generic term for cruising across Australia.

On 1 July 1985 *Oriana* hosted the King and Queen of Tonga, who visited the ship for a luncheon in honour of the King's 67th birthday.

Twenty-one days later, P&O announced that *Oriana*'s retirement was looming, with blame placed on a weak Australian dollar, which had impacted the ship's profitability. Her high operating costs, owing to her age and original ocean liner design, as well as the influx of cheap cruises on Soviet vessels, meant she was no longer competitive.

Oriana's last cruise took place in March 1986, with the ship returning to Sydney late that month. However, unlike her fleet mates, *Oriana* was not destined for the scrap heap; rather she was sold to Daiwa House KK in Japan for further use as a floating hotel.

The ship sailed for Japan on 29 May 1986, where she served in this role until the mid 1990s. She was then sold to Chinese owners and was relocated to Shanghai and later Dalian, where she was given a large-scale refit and reopened as a floating hotel again.

In 2004 the vessel was badly damaged by a severe storm, which caused her to take on water and partially capsize. This spelt the end for the vessel, and she was later sold for scrap in Zhangiagang, China.

Opposite: *Oriana* 1960–86 41,915grt. A final farewell. *Oriana* is towed out of Sydney Harbour, en route to her new owners in Japan – the unique *Oriana*, the last Orient liner and a remarkable testament to her breed, gone, but not forgotten. (Henderson/Cremer Collection, ref. OH6121)

In 1995 P&O introduced a new vessel to the British cruise market, named for the last of the Orient Line ships. The 1995-built *Oriana* will sail for P&O Cruises until August 2019. (Patricia Dempsey)

P&O Cruises' *Aurora* was built in 2000 and shares a name with one of the Orient Line Clipper Ships vessels. (Frame & Cross)

With *Oriana* broken up, the last of the Orient liners was gone. However, the legacy of this legendary shipping line survives to this day thanks to the P&O decision to name their 1995-built cruise ship *Oriana*.

The new *Oriana* is over 69,000 tons, and was the largest ship purpose-built for the British cruise market at that time. She was joined in 2000 by a near-sister ship, which carries the name *Aurora*, sharing the name of the Orient Line of Clipper Ships' vessel of 1874.

Both of these ships have developed a strong and loyal following. As P&O Cruises was itself acquired by Carnival Corporation in 2003 it no longer exists as an independent company, meaning the *Oriana* and *Aurora* are the last of their line, just as the *Oriana* of 1959 was the last of hers.

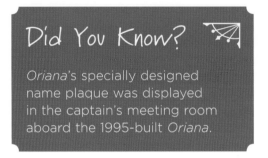

Did You Know?

Oriana's specially designed name plaque was displayed in the captain's meeting room aboard the 1995-built *Oriana*.

Sydney Harbour and its numerous coves and bays is the theme for this advertising piece by the British artist Herbert K. Rooke. (Henderson/Cremer ref. P&O_209)

MOSMAN BAY, SYDNEY HARBOUR

ORIENT LINE TO AUSTRALIA

via Gibraltar, South of France, Italy, Egypt & Ceylon.

CRUISES TO MEDITERRANEAN, CANARY ISLANDS, PALESTINE, NORWAY Etc.

Managers: ANDERSON, GREEN & Co. Ltd 5, Fenchurch Avenue, London, E.C.3.
West End Offices } 14, Cockspur Street, S.W.1. & No1, Australia House, Strand, W.C.2.

The Appeal of Venice

VENICE is one of the greatest attractions of Italy. Many travellers commence their continental tour at Naples, the first European port of call on the Orient Line route to London. After Rome and other fine Italian cities Venice, with its palaces and canals, its present beauties and memories of maritime greatness, is the fitting climax.

Travel to Europe by
ORIENT LINE

A 1930s advertisement enticing the Australian passenger to disembark at Naples and travel through Europe to London. The New Zealand born Albert Collins (1883–1951) undertook numerous commissions for the Orient Line. (Henderson/Cremer Collection, ref. 20014)

Paddy Boats, Negombo Canal

CEYLON

WITH a holiday of only a few weeks at your disposal, Ceylon is well within reach. It is an entirely new world to the traveller from the South. He is in the tropics yet enjoying a delightful climate. He will observe the strange customs and ceremonies of an interesting population; bazaars; native villages; ricefields; jungles and the ancient ruined cities they have over-run—all new to him and all of enthralling interest.

Ceylon Holiday Return Fares are very low.

ORIENT LINE

London

THE heart of the Empire calls to us all. Its immensity and variety of life, its beauty, wealth of art and historic associations, its pageantry, tradition and customs afford scope for never ending study.

Travel is the great educator and the Orient Line route to London is unsurpassed, offering as it does so many opportunities of observing the races and customs of other lands. The long experience of the Orient Line ensures that all travellers enjoy a pleasant and comfortable voyage.

Travel to England by

ORIENT LINE

From Walter Jardine comes this poster advertising travel on the Orient Line to London. Many Australians considered England 'home' even when they had never visited. (Henderson/Cremer Collection, ref. 20024)

Ceylon

November to January is the "Season" in Ceylon. Low Return Fares for Holiday Excursions • Reduced Rates for Round Eastern Tours—embracing

Ceylon
Singapore
and Java

in either direction.

Literature, including details of hotel and touring rates in Ceylon, will be sent on request.

WALTER JARDINE

ORIENT LINE

ORIENT STEAM NAVIGATION COMPANY LIMITED, INCORPORATED IN ENGLAND

Colombo in Ceylon (now Sri Lanka) was the first port of call after leaving Australia on the mail ships to England and the last port on the route before reaching Australia. The mail ships sailed weekly in each direction and Ceylon quickly became a popular holiday destination. Created by Walter Jardine. (Henderson/Cremer Collection, ref. 20083)

TRAVEL IN LUXURY

The comfortable cabin accommodation and the beautifully appointed Public Rooms on board the Orient Liners ensure the passenger of a most enjoyable voyage.

The First Class fares from Sydney to England ranges from £98 to £134 single and from £172 to £235 return.

ORIENT LINE

2 · 4 · 6 SPRING STREET · · SYDNEY

An image of *Orama* in the Suez Canal by Australian painter Albert Collins (1883–1951). The poster depicts the romance and mystique of the route with the powerful reassuring image of the *Orama*. (Henderson/Cremer Collection, ref. 40030)

A striking piece of Orient Line art incorporating a geometric art deco style advertising third-class travel. (Henderson/Cremer Collection, ref. folio 2_00723)

A typical art deco era design poster by the Australian artist Percy Trompf (1902–64) advertising third-class travel in the five 20,000-ton Orient Line steamers built in the 1920s. (Henderson/Cremer Collection, ref. folio 2_00751)

An Orient Line 1931 poster advertising the new one-class travel in the 1909 *Orsova* and *Ormonde*. Known as tourist steamers they provided a new offering alongside their more modern partners. (Henderson/Cremer Collection, ref. folio 2_00823)

ORIENT LINE
CRUISES TO
NORWAY
by
20,000 TON STEAMERS

Season
1926

From the beginning of its pioneering cruises in 1889 the Orient Line featured cruising to the Fjords of Norway, as depicted in this unsigned work of art for the 1926 season brochure. (Henderson/Cremer Collection ref. folio 1/00324)

LONDON

With the Compliments of
THE
ORIENT LINE

JOHN FARLEIGH

From the British engraver John Farleigh (1900–65) comes this piece of promotional art for London c. 1936, used by the Orient Line for first-class passengers. (Henderson/Cremer Collection, P&O_076)

ORIENT LINE CRUISES
BY 20,000 TON STEAMERS

NORWAY
& NORTHERN CAPITALS

An atmospheric, unsigned artwork produced for the Orient Line in the late 1920s, portraying the many scenes awaiting passengers on a cruise to the Norwegian fiords. (Henderson/Cremer Collection, ref. P&O_096)

Early steamships were fitted with auxillary sails to make use of favourable winds. (Frame & Cross)

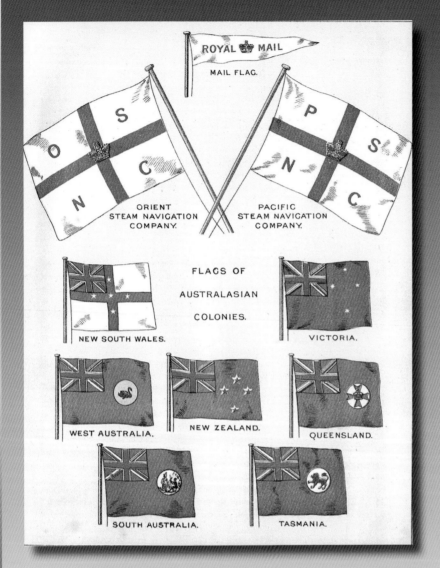

An Orient Line-issued poster showing the flags of the Orient and Pacific companies and the flags of the Australasian colonies. (Henderson/Cremer Collection)

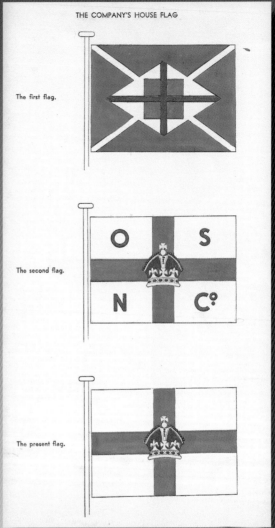

The three stages of the Orient Steam Navigation Line flag. It was initially a combination of the House flags of F. Green & Co., and the saltire of Anderson, Anderson & Co., the managers. It then developed in the style of the Pacific company flag with the quartered letters O.S.N. Co. and finally in 1909 the blue cross and crown standing alone. (Henderson/Cremer Collection, ref. OH10605)

APPENDIX 1

Orient Line of Clipper Ships

The following list of clipper ships owned or managed by Anderson, Anderson & Co., of London, (formerly James Thomson & Co.) to Australia was compiled from surviving company records and newspaper reports.

Henderson & Cremer Collection

Ship	Description	Australian Trade	Tonnage	Length	Beam	Depth of Hold
Orient	Composite ship, built for James Thomson & Co., by Thom. Bilbe & Co., Perry, Rotherhithe in 1853.	1856–77	1,183	184'4"	31'7"	21'1"
The Murray	Wooden ship, built for James Thomson & Co., by A. Hall & Co., of Aberdeen in 1861.	1861–79	903	205'	33'8"	20'6"
Coonatto	Composite ship, built for Anderson, Thomson & Co., by Thom. Bilbe & Co., Perry at Rotherhithe in 1863.	1863–75	633	160'2"	29'	18'7"
Goolwa	Composite ship, built for Anderson, Thomson & Co., by A. Hall of Aberdeen in 1865.	1864–84	717	178'5"	30'6"	18'8"
Red Riding Hood	Composite ship, built and owned by Thos. Bilbe & Co., Perry, Rotherhithe in 1857.	1865–76	720	185'	29'8"	20'
Yatala	Composite ship, built for Anderson, Thomson & Co., by Thos. Bilbe & Co., Rotherhithe in 1865.	1865–71	1,127	203'4"	34'6"	21'1"
White Eagle	Iron ship, built by A. Stephen & Sons of Glasgow in 1855. Purchased by Thomas Bilbe of Rotherhithe in 1865 and managed by Anderson, Anderson & Co.	1865–74	993	199'	31'4"	20'8"
Darra	Composite ship, built for Anderson, Thomson & Co., by J. Hall & Co., of Aberdeen, 1865.	1866–83	999	190'	33'5"	21'
Borealis	Composite ship, built by Thos. Bilbe of Rotherhithe in 1864 and managed by Anderson, Anderson & Co.	1868–83	920	205'	32'5"	21'
Kirkham	Iron ship, built for Jacob & Co., of Liverpool by J. Laird of Birkenhead in 1856. Purchased by Anderson, Anderson & Co., in 1870.	1870–79	1,061	201'	34'1"	12'6"

Ship	Description	Australian Trade	Tonnage	Length	Beam	Depth of Hold
Holmsdale	Wooden ship, built for Phillips & Co., of London by Reed of Sunderland in 1858. Purchased by Thos. Bilbe of Rotherhithe in 1872 and managed by Anderson, Anderson & Co.	1873–83	1,257	206'8"	37'7"	22'4"
Hesperus	Iron ship, built for Anderson, Anderson & Co., by Robert Steele & Co. of Greenock in 1873.	1873–99	1,777	262'2"	39'7"	25'
Pakwan	Composite ship, built for John Paton of London by Peverall of Sunderland in 1863. Purchased around 1874 by Capt. A. Lawrence and managed by Anderson, Anderson & Co.	1874–84	818	186'	32'5"	19'
Aurora	Composite ship, built for Anderson, Anderson & Co., by Robert Steele & Co. of Greenock in 1874.	1874–75	1,768	261'9"	39.5"	23'6"
Oaklands	Iron ship, built for A. Lawrence by Gourlay & Co., of Dundee in 1876 and managed by Anderson, Anderson & Co.	1876–86	1,013	203'8"	33'8'	19'
Harbinger	Iron ship, built for Anderson, Anderson & Co., by Robert Steele & Co. of Greenock in 1876.	1876–89	1,585	253'6"	37'6"	22'4"
Argonaut	Composite ship, built and owned by Thos. Bilbe & Wm. Perry of Rotherhithe, sold to Anderson, Anderson & Co., in 1877.	1877–83	1,073	206'	33'	26'

APPENDIX 2

Orient Steam Navigation Company

1877–1960

Fleet list of passenger ships, including chartered and partnered ships on the Orient Line schedule

Henderson & Cremer Collection

Ref.	Ship	Tonnage Gross/Net	Dimensions Length, Beam, Depth Feet-Metres	Specifications As Built	Capacity As Built First-Second-Third-Crew (where known)	Australian Service	Voyages to Australia	& Passengers Carried	Details
1	LUSITANIA	3,825 2,494	379.9'-41.3'-35.2' 115.79-12.59-10.73m	-- Launched 20 June 1871. --Yard No. 381. -- Official No. 65888. -- Builder, Laird Brothers, Birkenhead, England. -- Single screw, coal-fired two-cylinder compound engine made and installed by the builder, 550nhp, 15 knots. -- 146,120 cubic feet of cargo space. -- Built for £91,852.	74-76-265-105	1877-1900	37	11,106	Iron, barque rigged, clipper bow, rounded stern, one funnel, three masts. --1877: Chartered from Pacific Steam Navigation Co. --1877: Departed London 26 June on first voyage to Australia. --1878: Purchased by the newly formed Orient Steam Navigation Co., in May 1878 for £74,210. --1897: Final voyage to Australia from London 10 December, 1897, after which she undertook 'yachting cruises' from London. --1900: Sold to Pacific Steam Navigation Co. --1901: Sold to Elder, Dempster & Co., for £15,000. She was subsequently lost in the same year after going ashore at Cape Race on a voyage to Montreal. At the time she was under charter to Allan Line.
2	CHIMBORAZO	3,847 2,443	384'-41.3'-35.3' 117-12.59-10.76m	-- Launched 21 June 1871. -- Yard No. 128. -- Official No. 65886. -- Builder, John Elder & Co., Govan, Scotland. -- Iron, single screw, coal-fired two-cylinder compound engine made by and installed by the builder, 550nhp, 13 knots. -- 146,120 cubic feet of cargo space.	72-92-265-105	1877-94	24	8,604	Iron, barque rigged, clipper bow, rounded stern, one funnel, three masts --1877: Chartered from Pacific Steam Navigation Co. --1877: Departed London 12 August, 1877 on her first voyage to Australia. --1878: Purchased by the newly formed Orient Steam Navigation Co., in August 1878 for £72,270. --1887: Departed London 12 May on final voyage to Australia. --1894: Sold to P.J. Pitcher of Liverpool as a cruise ship named *Cleopatra* under ownership of Ocean Cruising and Highland Yachting Co. --1897: Sold to Thomas W. Ward and broken up at Preston.
3	CUZCO	3,845 2,437	384.2'-41.4'-35.3' 117.1-12.6-10.76m	--Launched 18 October 1871. --Yard No. 129. --Official No. 65901. --Builder, John Elder & Co., Govan, Scotland. --Iron single screw, coal-fired three-cylinder compound engine made and installed by the builder, 550nhp, 13 knots.	74-76-265-105	1877-1905	62	15,475	Iron, barque rigged, clipper bow, rounded stern, one funnel, three masts. --1877: Chartered from Pacific Steam Navigation Co. --1877: Departed London 25 September on her first voyage to Australia. --1878: Purchased by the newly formed Orient Steam Navigation Co., on 3 March 1878 for £78,150. --1902: Departed London 23 May 1902 on final voyage to Australia. --1905: Sold to Luigi Pittaluga of Genoa and broken up.

Ref.	Ship	Tonnage Gross/Net	Dimensions Length, Beam, Depth Feet-Metres	Specifications As Built	Capacity As Built First-Second-Third-Crew (where known)	Australian Service	Voyages to Australia	& Passengers Carried	Details
4	STAD AMSTERDAM	2,920 1,720	349.7'-38.4'-28' 106.59-11.7-8.5m	--Launched 10 December 1874. --Builder, A. & J. Inglis Ltd, Glasgow. --Iron single screw, two-cylinder engine, 450hp.		1877	1	249	Owing to some repairs required on the *Garonne*, the line chartered the *Stad Amsterdam* for one voyage return voyage only in 1877 from Royal Netherlands Steamship Co., departing London 24 October 1877.
5	GARONNE	3,876 2,468	382.1'-41.4'-35.7' 116.5-12.6-10.89m	--Launched 22 April 1871. --Yard No. 152. --Official No. 65855. --Builder, Robert Napier & Sons, Glasgow, Scotland. --Iron, single screw, coal-fired two-cylinder compound engine made and installed by the builder, 624nhp, 13 knots. -- 146,120 cubic feet of cargo space.	70-86-265	1878-98	25	8,575	Iron, barque rigged, clipper bow, rounded stern, one funnel, three masts. --1877: Chartered from Pacific Steam Navigation Co. --1878: Departed London 17 April 1878 on her first voyage to Australia and the first ship registered in the ownership of the Orient Steam Navigation Co. --1878: Purchased by the newly formed Orient Steam Navigation Co., for £71,570. --1889: Departed London 7 June 1889 on final voyage to Australia. --1898: Sold to F. Waterhouse Ltd, Seattle for $9,500, she retained the name *Garonne* and was used in the Alaskan gold rush and served as troopship to the Philippines during the Spanish–American War. --1905: Broken up at Genoa.
6	ACONCAGUA	4,106 2,639	404.8'-41.4'-35.3' 123.38-12.6-10.76m	--Launched 6 June 1872. --Yard No. 130. --Official No. 65969. --Builder, John Elder & Co., Govan, Scotland. --Coal-fired two-cylinder compound engine made and installed by the builder, 600nhp, 13 knots. -- 161,460 cubic feet of cargo space.	126-40-800-112	1878-81	7	2,667	Auxiliary steamer, iron hull, clipper bow, single screw, one funnel, three masts, originally barque rigged with yards on the main and striking top gallant masts. -- Pacific Steam Navigation Co. ship operating on the Australian service in partnership with the Orient Line. --1878: First voyage to Australia from London, 17 May 1878. --1881: Final voyage to Australia from London, 11 May 1881. --1895: Sold to Verdeau et Compagnie, of Bordeaux, and renamed *Egypte*. --1896: Sold and broken up.
7	JOHN ELDER	3,832 2,431	381.9'-41.5'-35.2' 116.4-12.64-10.72m	--Launched 29 August 1870. --Yard No. 110. --Official No. 63313. --Builder, John Elder & Co., Govan, Scotland. --Coal-fired two-cylinder compound engine made and installed by the builder, 550nhp, 12 knots.	72-92-265	1879-86	19	6,868	Auxiliary steamer, iron hull, clipper bow, single screw, two funnels, three masts with yards on fore and main. --Pacific Steam Navigation Co. ship operating on the Australian service in partnership with the Orient Line. --1879: First voyage to Australia from London, 27 January 1879. --1886: Final voyage to Australia from London, 27 May 1886. --1892: Lost after striking rocks off Cape Carranza, Chile.
8	COTOPAXI	4,028 2,583	402.2'-42.8'-34.3' 122.59-13.04-10.45m	--Launched 15 March 1873. --Yard No. 146. --Official No. 69265. --Builder, John Elder & Co., Govan, Scotland. --Coal-fired two-cylinder compound engine made and installed by the builder, 600nhp, 12 knots.	136-41-800	1880-82	9	2,495	Iron hull, auxiliary steamer, clipper bow, single screw, one funnel, three masts, originally barque rigged with yards on the main and striking topgallant masts. --Pacific Steam Navigation Co. ship operating on the Australian service in partnership with the Orient Line. --1880: First voyage to Australia from London, 14 April 1880. --1882: Final voyage to Australia from London, 12 August 1882. Was to have completed another voyage in December 1882 but this was cancelled after she caught fire whilst loading cargo in London. --1889: On a voyage from England to Valparaiso the *Cotopaxi* was beached after a collision with the steamer *Olympia*. Refloated *Cotopaxi* struck rocks and foundered in Messier Channel, no lives were lost.

Ref.	Ship	Tonnage Gross/Net	Dimensions Length, Beam, Depth Feet-Metres	Specifications As Built	Capacity As Built First-Second-Third-Crew (where known)	Australian Service	Voyages to Australia	Passengers Carried	Details
9	CITY OF LONDON	2,560 2,097	381.6'-38.8'-29' 116.31-11.82-8.84m	--Launched 1876. --Yard No. 122. --Official No. 73818. --Builder, Charles Connell & Co., Whiteinch, Glasgow, Scotland. --Coal-fired two-cylinder inverted compound engine made by J. & J. Thomson, Glasgow, 450nhp, 11 knots. --Built for George Smith & Sons, 200 Argyle St, Glasgow.		1879	1	483	Iron hull, auxiliary steamer, single screw. --Chartered from G. Smith & Sons, Glasgow, Scotland, (City Line) for one voyage only to Australia, passengers embarked at London on 30 June 1879.
10	SULTAN	2,502 1,890	319'-37.6'-27.7' 97.23-11.46-8.44m	--Launched 1873. --Official No. 68432. --Builder, Green & Co., Blackwall, England. --Coal-fired two-cylinder, inverted direct acting compound engine made by Ravenhill, Eastons & Co., London, 240nhp, 12 knots. --Built For, R. & H. Green		1879	1	325	Iron hull, auxiliary steamer, single screw. --Chartered from R. & H. Green & Co., for one voyage only to Australia from London on 28 July 1879.
11	ORIENT	5,386 3,231	445.6'-46.3'-35.1' 135.82-14.11-10.69m	--Launched 5 June 1879. --Yard No. 224. --Official No. 82254. --Builder John Elder & Co., Govan, Scotland. --Coal-fired three-cylinder compound engine made by the builder, 5,000ihp, 15 knots. --Fitted with 35,113 cubic feet of refrigerated space. --Built for £148,400.	120-130-300-150	1879-1910	68	25,354	Iron hull, auxiliary steamer, straight stem, single screw, two funnels, four masts, fore and main rigged with yards. Four decks. --First passenger steamship built for the Orient Steam Navigation Company's Australian service. --1879: First voyage to Australia from London, 1 November 1879 in the record time to Adelaide of 37 days and 22 hours. --1882: Chartered for two months for service as a troopship during the uprising in Egypt. --1909: Departed London 23 July 1909 on final voyage to Australia. --1910: Sold to Luigi Pittaluga, Genoa for £12,500 and broken up in Genoa, Italy. On her delivery voyage to Genoa the *Orient* was renamed *Oric*.
12	SORATA	4,014 2,573	401.3'-42.8'-34.1' 122.32-13.04-10.39m	--Launched 2 October 1872. --Yard No. 144. --Official No. 65991. --Builder, John Elder & Co., Govan, Scotland. --Coal-fired two-cylinder compound engine made by the builder, 600nhp, 12 knots.	140-50-800	1880-86	15	5,297	Auxiliary steamer, iron hull, clipper bow, single screw, one funnel, three masts, originally barque rigged with yards on the main and striking topgallant masts. --Pacific Steam Navigation Co., ship operating on the Australian service in partnership with the Orient Line. --1880: First voyage to Australia from London, 13 February. --1886: Final voyage to Australia from London, 29 April. --1895: Sold to Thirkell & Co., Liverpool and broken up at Tranmere.
13	LIGURIA	4,666 2,980	433.4'-45'-34.1' 132.1-13.71-10.39m	--Launched 18 February 1874. --Yard No. 161. --Official No. 69367. --Builder, John Elder & Co., Govan, Scotland. --Coal-fired three-cylinder compound engine made by the builder, 750nhp, 4,000ihp, 13 knots.	100-150-340	1880-90	28	10,475	Iron hull auxiliary steamer, clipper bow, single screw, two funnels, three masts with yards on fore and main. --Pacific Steam Navigation Co., ship operating on the Australian service in partnership with the Orient Line. --1880: First voyage to Australia from London, 12 May. --1890: Final voyage to Australia from London, 6 May. --1903: Sold to F. Bruzzo of Genoa and broken up at Genoa, Italy.
14	POTOSI	4,219 2,704	421.6'-43.3'-33.5' 128.5-13.19-10.21m	--Launched 14 May 1873. --Yard No. 157. --Official No. 69278. --Builder, John Elder & Co., Govan, Scotland. --Iron single screw, coal-fired two-cylinder compound engine made by the builder, 600nhp, 13 knots.	136-41-800	1880-87	19	7,937	Iron hull auxiliary steamer, clipper bow, single screw, two funnels, three masts with yards on fore and main. --Pacific Steam Navigation Co., ship operating on the Australian service in partnership with the Orient Line. --1880: First voyage to Australia from London, 7 July 1880. --1887: Final voyage to Australia from London, 26 May 1887. --1897: Sold and broken up at Genoa, Italy.

Ref.	Ship	Tonnage Gross/Net	Dimensions Length, Beam, Depth Feet-Metres	Specifications As Built	Capacity As Built First-Second-Third-Crew (where known)	Australian Service	Voyages to Australia	& Passengers Carried	Details
15	AUSTRAL	5,589 3,271	456'-48.2'-33.9' 138.9-14.69-10.33m	--Launched 24 December 1881. --Yard No. 249. --Official No. 85923. --Builder, John Elder & Co., Govan, Scotland. --Coal-fired three-cylinder compound engine, made by the builder, 1,000nhp, 17 knots. --Fitted with 57,791 cubic feet of refrigerated space. --When built, could spread 28,000 square feet of sail on her four masts.	120-130-300	1882-1903	53	18,824	Mild steel auxiliary steamer, single screw, two funnels, four masts, straight stem, elliptical stern, rigged for square sail on fore and main, fore and aft on mizzen and jigger. --Second passenger steamship built for the Orient Steam Navigation Company's Australian service. --1882: Sailed on maiden voyage from London, 19 May for Australia --1882: Sank on 11 November whilst coaling at Neutral Bay in Sydney. --1884: Chartered by the Anchor Line for seven return voyages from Liverpool to New York. --1900: Served as a Boer War Transport. --1902: Final voyage to Australia from London 21 November. --1903: Sold to the Italian firm of Gastaldi, Genoa for £13,250 and broken up.
16	CEPHALONIA	5,517 3,490	430.6'-46.5'-34.5' 131.24-14.14-10.51m	--Launched 20 May 1882. --Builder Laird Brothers, Birkenhead, England. --Coal-fired two-cylinder inverted compound engines made by the builder, 4,000ihp, 14 knots.	200-nil-1500	1883	1	646	Iron hull, barque rigged, straight stem, single screw, one funnel, three masts with yards on fore and main. --Chartered from the Cunard Line for one return voyage only to Australia. --One emigrant voyage only from London on 12 January 1883 with 646 emigrants for Sydney.
17	IBERIA	4,671 2,982	433.5'-45'-34.1' 132.13-13.71-10.39 m	--Launched 6 December 1873. --Yard No. 162. --Official No. 69336. --Builder, John Elder & Co., Govan, Scotland. --Coal-fired three-cylinder compound engine made by the builder, 75nhp, 16.5 knots.	140-50-800-150	1882-90	20	8,043	Iron hull auxiliary steamer, clipper bow, single screw, two funnels, three masts with yards on fore and main. --Pacific Steam Navigation Co., ship operating on the Australian service in partnership with the Orient Line. --1882: Chartered for five months for service as a troopship during the uprising in Egypt. --1883: First voyage to Australia from London, 25 January. --1889: Iberia was the first Orient Line steamer to call at Hobart on 25 March. --1890: Final voyage to Australia from London, 31 January. --1903: Sold and broken up at Genoa.
18	ORIZABA	6,184 3,587	460'-49.3'-19.4' 140.2-15.02-5.91m	--Launched 6 May 1886. --Yard No. 138. --Official No. 93688. --Builder, Barrow Shipbuilding Co., Barrow in-Furness, England. --Coal-fired three-cylinder triple-expansion engine made by the builder, 1,200nhp, 7,000ihp, 16.5 knots. --Fitted with 44,500 cubic feet of refrigerated space.	126-154-412	1886-1905	55	17,375	Steel hull, straight stem, single screw, four decks, two funnels, elliptical stern, four masts with yards on fore which were removed in 1890. --Pacific Steam Navigation Co., ship operating on the Australian service in partnership with the Orient Line. --1886: First voyage to Australia from London, 30 September. --1905: On a voyage from London to Australia the Orizaba ran aground off Fremantle, Garden Island on Five Fathom Bank on 17 February and was lost.
19	ORMUZ	6,031 2,940	465.5'-52.1'-34.1' 14'.88-15.88-10.39m	--Launched 29 September 1886. --Yard No. 317. --Official No. 93341. --Builder, Fairfield Shipbuilding & Engineering Co., Ltd, Glasgow, Scotland. --Coal-fired three-cylinder triple-expansion Engine made by the builder, 1,400nhp, 9,000ihp, 18 knots. --Fitted with 44,501 cubic feet of refrigerated space.	168-168-300	1886-1912	70	26,310	Mild steel, single screw, barque, five decks, two funnels, four masts, straight stem, elliptical stern, rigged for square sail on fore and main. --Third passenger steamship built for the Orient Steam Navigation Company's Australian service. --First Orient liner to be built with triple-expansion engines. --1887: Departed London on 3 February on her maiden voyage to Australia. --1889: Represented the Orient Line at the Royal Navy Spithead Review on 3 August, 1889. --1911: Final voyage to Australia from London on 18 August. --1912: Sold to Compagnie de Navigation Sud-Atlantique for £19,000 and renamed Divona. --1922: Broken up.

Ref.	Ship	Tonnage Gross/Net	Dimensions Length, Beam, Depth Feet-Metres	Specifications As Built	Capacity As Built First-Second-Third- Crew (where known)	Australian Service	Voyages to Australia	& Passengers Carried	Details
20	OROYA	6,057 3,266	460'-49.3'-35.3' 140.2-15.02-10.76m	--Launched 31 August 1886. --Yard No. 139. --Official No. 93712. --Builder, Barrow Shipbuilding Co., Barrow-in-Furness, England. --Coal-fired three-cylinder triple-expansion engine, 1,200nhp, 7,000ihp, 16.5 knots. --Fitted with 44,500 cubic feet of refrigerated space.	126-154-412	1887-1909	64	19,615	Steel hull, straight stem, single screw, four decks, two funnels, elliptical stern, four masts with yards on fore. --Pacific Steam Navigation Co., ship operating on the Australian service in partnership with the Orient Line. --1887: First voyage to Australia from London, 17 February. --1895: On 4 March the Oroya ran ashore off Naples. On being refloated she went to Belfast for repairs. --1906: Acquired by the Royal Mail Steam Packet Co. --1909: Final voyage to Australia from London. --1909: Broken up.
21	OROTAVA	5,552 3,096	430'-49.3'-34.2' 131.06-15.02-10.42m	--Launched 15 June 1889. --Yard No. 166. --Official No. 96348. --Builder, The Naval Construction and Armament Co., Barrow-in-Furness, England. --Coal-fired three-cylinder triple-expansion engine made by the builder, 1,030nhp, 7,000ihp, 16.5 knots. --Fitted with 40,000 cubic feet of refrigerated space.	126-120-400	1890-1909	46	10,704	Steel hull, straight stem, single screw, four decks, two funnels, elliptical stern, four masts with the main and mizzen removed in 1906. --Pacific Steam Navigation Co., ship operating on the Australian service in partnership with the Orient Line. --1890: First voyage to Australia from London, 6 June. --1896: Sank in December whilst coaling at Tilbury. --1899–1903: Chartered as troopship during the Boer War. --1905: Orotava first Orient Line arrival in Brisbane on 2 September. --1906: Acquired by the Royal Mail Steam Packet Co. --1909: Final voyage to Australia from London, 5 March. --1914: Requisitioned as armed merchant cruiser in World War I. --1915: Sold to the British Admiralty. --1919: Troopship service then sold for demolition.
22	ORUBA	5,552 3,096	430'-49.3'-34.2' 131.06-15.02-10.42m	--Launched 20 March 1889. --Yard No. 165. --Official No. 96310. --Builder, The Naval Construction and Armament Co., Barrow-in-Furness, England. --Coal-fired three-cylinder triple-expansion engine made and installed by the builder, 1,030nhp, 7,000ihp, 16 knots. --Fitted with 40,000 cubic feet of refrigerated space.	126-120-400	1890-1905	51	14,274	Steel hull, straight stem, single screw, four decks, two funnels, elliptical stern, four masts with the main and mizzen removed in 1906. --Pacific Steam Navigation Co., ship operating on the Australian service in partnership with the Orient Line. --1890: First voyage to Australia from London 4 July. --1906: Acquired by the Royal Mail Steam Packet Co. --1908: Final voyage to Australia from London 16 October. --1914: In World War I sold to the British Admiralty and converted into a dummy battleship at Harland & Wolff. --1916: Scuttled as breakwater in the Aegean at Kephalo Bay.
23	OPHIR	6,910 3,223	465'-53.4'-34.1' 141.73-16.27-10.39m	--Launched 11 April 1891. --Yard No. 421. --Official No. 98673. --Builder, Robert Napier & Sons, Glasgow, Scotland. --Coal-fired three-cylinder triple-expansion engine made and installed by the builder, 1,734nhp, 10,000ihp, 18 knots. --Fitted with 52,400 cubic feet of refrigerated space.	222-150-500	1891-1918	51	19,234	Steel, twin screw, two funnels, two masts, straight stem, elliptical stern. --Fourth passenger steamship built for the Orient Steam Navigation Company's Australian service. --1891: Departed London 6 November on maiden voyage to Australia. --1901: The Ophir was used as Royal Yacht HMY Ophir for a tour of the Empire with T.R.H. Duke and Duchess of Cornwall and York on board. --1913: Final voyage to Australia from London 20 June. --1915: Commissioned as Armed Merchant Cruiser; subsequently sold to the Royal Navy for £25,000. --1921/22: Sold by the Admiralty and broken up at Troon.
24	OMRAH	8,291 4,632	490.7'-56.7'-34.2' 149.56-17.28-10.42m	--Launched 3 September 1898. --Yard No. 404. --Official No. 108782. --Builder, Fairfield Shipbuilding & Engineering Co., Glasgow, Scotland. --Coal-fired three-cylinder triple-expansion engine made and installed by the builder, 1,350nhp, 9,200ihp, 18 knots. --Fitted with 77,000 cubic feet of refrigerated space. --Built for £215,000 (approx.)	161-162-500	1899-1918	55	22,361	Steel, twin screw, one funnel, two masts, straight stem, elliptical stern. --Fifth passenger steamship built for the Orient Steam Navigation Company's Australian service. --1899: Departed London 3 February on maiden voyage to Australia. --1914: Requisitioned by Australian Government for service as troopship No. A5. Commonwealth control ended on 10 February 1915. --1917: Requisitioned as troopship and in April was taken under the control of Liner Requisition Scheme. --1918: On 12 May torpedoed by UB-52 and lost off Cape Spartivento, Sardinia. One life and the mails were lost.

Ref.	Ship	Tonnage Gross/Net	Dimensions Length, Beam, Depth Feet-Metres	Specifications As Built	Capacity As Built First-Second-Third-Crew (where known)	Australian Service	Voyages to Australia	Passengers Carried	Details
25	ORTONA	7,945 4,115	500'-55.3'-33.7' 152.4-16.85-10.27m	--Launched 10 July 1899. --Yard No. 272. --Official No. 110613. --Builder, Vickers Sons and Maxim Ltd, Barrow-in-Furness, England. --Twin screw, coal-fired, two three-cylinder triple-expansion engines, 1,750nhp, 10,000ihp, 18 knots.	140-180-300	1899-1906	27	10,189	--Pacific Steam Navigation Co., ship operating on the Australian service in partnership with the Orient Line. --1899: First voyage to Australia from London 24 November. --1902: Requisitioned as transport during the Boer War. --1906: Acquired by the Royal Mail Steam Packet Co. --1909: Final voyage to Australia from London 30 April. --1910: Converted to cruise ship *Arcadian*. --1917: Torpedoed on 15 April by UC-74 and lost near the Greek Island of Milo whilst carrying troops; 277 lives were lost.
26	VICTORIA	5,549 3,742	401'4'-52'3'-26'2' 121.5-15.8-7.9m	--Launched 21 June 1902. --Official No. 115316. --Builder, Fairfield and Co., Ltd, Glasgow. --Twin screw, coal-fired, triple-expansion engines, 13.5 knots.	106-104-595	1902	1	105	--Pacific Steam Navigation Co., ship operating on the Australian service in partnership with the Orient Line for one return voyage only from London 12 September 1902.
27	ORONTES	9,023 4,622	513.7'-58.2'-34.5' 156.57-17.74-10.52m	--Launched 10 May 1902. --Yard No. 418. --Official No. 115707. --Builder, Fairfield Shipbuilding & Engineering Co., Ltd, Glasgow, Scotland. --Twin screw, coal-fired two quadruple-expansion four-cylinder engines made and installed by the builder, 1,700thp, 10,000ihp, 18 knots. --Fitted with 69,533 cubic feet of refrigerated space.	152-147-368	1902-22	56	23,594	Steel, six decks, twin screw, one funnel, two masts, straight stem, elliptical stern. --Sixth passenger steamship built for the Orient Steam Navigation Company's Australian service. --1902: First voyage to Australia from London 24 October. --During World War I *Orontes* served as both a freight and troop transport ship. --1921: Final voyage to Australia from London 19 February. --1921: Laid up for a time and then sold for the use as a British Trade and Exhibition ship, a role which never eventuated. --1926: Sold and finally broken up at Inverkeithing.
28	ORITA	9,231		--Launched 1902. --Builder, Harland & Wolff, Belfast. --Twin screw quadruple-expansion engines, 14 knots.		1901		258	--Pacific Steam Navigation Co., ship operating on the Australian service in partnership with the Orient Line for one voyage only from London 8 May 1903.
29	MILTIADES	6,793	512'-55'-26.11' 152.7-16.7-7.9m	--Launched 11 August 1903. --Yard No. 401. --Builder, Alexander Stephen & Sons, Glasgow. --Twin screw, 15 knots.	89-nil-158	1907	1	481	--Twin screw, clipper bow, one funnel, two masts.
30	ASTURIAS	12,002	535'-62'-31' 163.06-18.89-9.45m	--Launched 26 September 1907. --Yard No. 388. --Official no. 124669. --Builder, Harland & Wolff, Belfast --Twin screw, quadruple-expansion engines, 15 knots.	300-14-1200	1908-09	2	1,318	--Pacific Steam Navigation Co., ship operating on the Australian service in partnership with the Orient Line. --First voyage to Australia from London 24 January 1908. --Final voyage to Australia from London 5 February 1909.

Ref.	Ship	Tonnage Gross/Net	Dimensions Length, Beam, Depth Feet-Metres	Specifications As Built	Capacity As Built First-Second-Third- Crew (where known)	Australian Service	Voyages to Australia	& Passengers Carried	Details
31	ORSOVA	12,036 6,831	536.2'-63.3'-34.3' 163.43-19.29-10.45m	--Launched 07 November 1908. --Yard No. 383. --Official No. 128278. --Builder, John Brown & Co., Ltd, Clydebank, Scotland. --Coal-fired quadruple-expansion four-cylinder engines made and installed by the builder, 1,987nhp, 14,000ihp, 18 knots. --Fitted with 88,250 cubic feet of refrigerated space.	287-126-660-291 From 1933 660 Tourist Class	1909-36	73	47,575	Steel, twin screw, schooner rigged, three decks, five holds, two funnels, two masts, straight stem, elliptical stern. --Seventh passenger steamship built for the Orient Steam Navigation Company's Australian service. --1909: Departed London 25 June on maiden voyage to Australia. --1915: Chartered as troopship, World War I. --1917: Struck a mine laid by UC-68 and successfully beached in Cawsand Bay on 14 March; refloated and repaired at Devonport. --1918: Requisitioned and used as troopship. --1919: Released from government service. --1919: First post-war commercial voyage to Australia from London on 22 November. --1936: Final voyage to Australia from London 20 June. --1936: Sold and broken up at Bo'ness.
32	OTWAY	12,077 6,690	535.9'-63.2'-34.2' 163.34-19.26-10.42m	--Launched 21 November 1908. --Yard No. 459. --Official No. 128282. --Builder, Fairfield Shipbuilding & Engineering Co., Ltd, Glasgow, Scotland. --Coal-fired, two quadruple-expansion four-cylinder engine made and installed by the builder, 1,700nhp, 10,000ihp, 18 knots. --Fitted with 91,000 cubic feet of refrigerated space.	280-115-700	1909-17	17	13,546	Steel, twin screw, schooner rigged, three decks, five holds, two funnels, two masts, straight stem, elliptical stern. --Eighth passenger steamship built for the Orient Steam Navigation Company's Australian service. --1909: Departed London 9 July on maiden voyage to Australia. --1914: Requisitioned by the British Admiralty for service as armed merchant cruiser in the Tenth Cruiser Squadron, armed with eight 6in and two 6-pound guns. --1917: Torpedoed by UC-49 on 22 July, north of the Butt of Lewis, ten lives were lost.
33	OSTERLEY	12,129 6,781	535'-63.2'-34.1' 163.06-19.26-10.39m	--Launched 26 January 1909. --Yard No. 333. --Official No. 128287. --Builder, the London and Glasgow Engineering and Shipbuilding Co., Ltd, Govan, Scotland. --Coal-fired two quadruple-expansion four-cylinder engines made and installed by the builder, 1,973nhp, 14,000ihp, 18 knots. --Fitted with 92,940 cubic feet of refrigerated space.	282-130-688	1909-30	57	43,107	Steel, twin screw, schooner rigged, three decks, five holds, two funnels, two masts, straight stem, elliptical stern. --Ninth passenger steamship built for the Orient Steam Navigation Company's Australian service. --1909: The launching ceremony took place on 21 January as planned, however the day was cold and the tallow on the slips had frozen. Despite all efforts Osterley refused to move until five days later when fresh tallow and efforts were successful in launching her. --1909: Departed London 6 August on maiden voyage to Australia. --1909: Collided at Port Said with the Russian steamer Roman and damaged. --1917: Taken under the World War I Liner Requisition Scheme. --1919: First post-World War I commercial voyage to Australia from London on 27 September. --1922: Chartered for three Norwegian cruises by a New York-based Tourist Agency. --1924: Stranded in the Brisbane River. --1929: Final voyage to Australia from London 3 August. --1930: Sold to P. and W. Maclellan, Glasgow for £26,000 and broken up at Bo'ness.

Ref.	Ship	Tonnage Gross/Net	Dimensions Length, Beam, Depth Feet-Metres	Specifications As Built	Capacity As Built First-Second-Third-Crew (where known)	Australian Service	Voyages to Australia	Passengers Carried	Details
34	OTRANTO	12,124 7,433	535.3'-64'-38.6' 163.16-19.50-11.76m	--Launched 27 March 1909. --Yard No. 278. --Official No. 124675. --Builder, Workman, Clark & Co., Ltd, Belfast. --Coal-fired, two quadruple-expansion four-cylinder engines made and installed by the builder, 1,976nhp, 14,000ihp, 18 knots. --Fitted with 95,000 cubic feet of refrigerated space.	235-186-696	1909-18	16	11,262	Steel, twin screw, schooner rigged, three decks, five holds, two funnels, two masts, straight stem, elliptical stern. --Tenth passenger steamship built for the Orient Steam Navigation Company's Australian service. --1909: Departed London 1 October on her maiden Australian voyage. --1914: Requisitioned by the British Admiralty for service as armed merchant cruiser HMS Otranto. --1916: Arrived in Sydney on 14 January after a lengthy voyage from South America. --1918: While in convoy from New York with American troops on board the Otranto, on 6 October collided with the P&O transport Kashmir. Severely damaged she went ashore on Islay, Scotland and broke up; 431 lives were lost.
35	ORVIETO	12,130 7,421	535.3'-64'-38.6' 163.16-19.50-11.76m	--Launched 6 July 1909. --Yard No. 279. --Official No. 129628. --Builder, Workman, Clark & Co., Ltd, Belfast. --Coal-fired, two quadruple-expansion four-cylinder engines made and installed by the builder, 1,976nhp, 14,000ihp, 18 knots. --Fitted with 95,000 cubic feet of refrigerated space.	235-186-696	1909-31	47	39,000	Steel, twin screw, schooner rigged, three decks, five holds, two funnels, two masts, straight stem, elliptical stern. --Eleventh passenger steamship built for the Orient Steam Navigation Company's Australian service. --Named after the Italian city in Umbria. --1909: Departed London 26 November on maiden voyage to Australia. --1914: Requisitioned by Australian Government for service as troopship A3. Commonwealth control ended on 29 December 1914. --1915: Requisitioned by the British Admiralty for service as armed merchant cruiser HMS Orvieto in the Tenth Cruiser Squadron. --1919: First post-World War I commercial voyage to Australia from London on 1 November. --1930: Final voyage to Australia from London 30 August. --1931: Sold to P. & W. MacLellan Ltd, and broken up at Bo'ness.
36	ORAMA	12,927 8,179	551'-64.2'-39' 167.94-19.56-11.89m	--Launched 28 June 1911. --Yard No. 403. --Official No. 132989. --Builder, John Brown & Co., Ltd, Clydebank, Scotland. --Coal-fired, two triple-expansion four-cylinder engines plus low-pressure turbine made and installed by the builder, 1,987nhp, 14,000ihp, 18 knots. --Fitted with 97,817 cubic feet of refrigerated space.	240-210-630	1911-17	10	8,732	Steel, triple screw, schooner rigged, three decks, five holds, two funnels, two masts, straight stem, elliptical stern. --Twelfth passenger steamship built for the Orient Steam Navigation Company's Australian service. --1911: Departed London 10 November on maiden voyage to Australia. --1914: World War I, requisitioned in September by the British Admiralty as the armed merchant cruiser HMS Orama. --1917: Torpedoed on 19 October by U-62 and lost in the North Atlantic, 210 miles off Scilly Isles.
37	ORMONDE	14,852 9,021	580.5'-66.7'-40.5' 176.93-20.33-12.34m	--Keel laid, May 1913. --Launched 10 February 1917. --Yard No. 425. --Official No. 141866. --Builder, John Brown & Co., Ltd, Clydebank, Scotland. --Six coal-burning Brown-Curtis geared steam turbines made and installed by the builder, 2,120nhp, 15,000ihp, 18 knots. -- Fitted with 101,635 cubic feet of refrigerated space. --Converted to oil burning in 1923.	278-196-1,017 From 1933 Tourist Class: 777 From 1947 Immigrants: 1,050	1917-52	76	64,0C5	Steel, twin screw, schooner rigged, five decks, seven holds, two funnels, two masts, straight stem, cruiser stern. --Thirteenth passenger steamship built for the Orient Steam Navigation Company's Australian service. --1917: Requisitioned in October as troop transport. --1931: Converted to tourist/one-class ship in 1931. --1936: A spontaneous fire broke out in a cargo of coir which had been loaded in Colombo. The ship was off the South Coast of New South Wales and put into Eden Harbour until the fire was extinguished; repaired in Sydney. --1939: World War II, requisitioned as troop transport. --1947: Refitted for commercial service by Cammell Laird & Co., Ltd. --1947: Departed London 10 October on first voyage to Australia as an emigrant ship. 1952: Final voyage to Australia from London on 21 August. Sold to British Iron and Steel Corp., and broken up at Troon.

Ref.	Ship	Tonnage Gross/Net	Dimensions Length, Beam, Depth Feet-Metres	Specifications As Built	Capacity As Built First-Second-Third-Crew (where known)	Australian Service	Voyages to Australia & Passengers Carried	Details
38	INDARRA	9,735	451'-60'-37' 137.46-18.29-11.27m	--Launched 1912. --Builder, Wm Denny, Dumbarton --Twin screw, quadruple-expansion engines, 13 knots.		1919	2 / 1,179	--Chartered by the Orient Line from the Australian United Steam Navigation Co. to augment their Australian service due to war losses. --1919: First voyage to Australia as an Orient liner on 20 December. --1920: After her second voyage, which departed London on 1 May, she was deemed too slow for the Orient Line service and her third voyage was undertaken by *Königin Luise*.
39	OMAR	10,711 6,790	523.1'-60.1'-34.9' 159.44-18.32-10.63m	--Launched 17 October 1896 as *Königin Luise*. --Yard No. 232. --Official No. 143196. --Builder, A.G. Vulcan, Stettin, Germany for Norddeutscher Lloyd's New York service. --Twin screw, coal-fired quadruple-expansion four-cylinder engines made and installed by the builder, 846nhp, 6,000ihp, 13.5 knots.	70-nil-757	1920-24	11 / 10,239	--1919: War reparation ship handed over to the British after World War I, to the Shipping Controller with Orient Line as managers. --1920: Purchased by Orient Line in August. --1920: First voyage to Australia as an Orient liner from London 4 September, she was still named *Königin Luise*. Renamed *Omar* after this voyage. --1924: Final voyage to Australia from London 9 February. --1924: Sold to Byron Steamship Co., Ltd, London and renamed *Edison*. --1935: Broken up at Genoa.
40	ORCADES	9,764 5,704	492'-57.6'-35' 149.96-17.55-10.66m	--Launched 12 May 1906 as *Prinz Ludwig*. --Yard No. 265. --Official No. 143122. --Builder, A.G. Vulcan, Stettin, Germany for Norddeutscher Lloyd Far East service. --Twin screw, coal-fired quadruple-expansion four-cylinder engines made and installed by the builder, 836nhp, 7,000ihp, 15 knots.	123-nil-476	1921-25	5 / 2,836	--1919: War reparation ship handed over to the British after World War I, to the Shipping Controller with P&O S.N. Co., as managers. --1921: Purchased by Orient Line in March and renamed *Orcades*. --1921: First voyage to Australia as an Orient liner from London 8 October. --1924: Final voyage to Australia from London 20 September. --1925: Sold to M. Stern, A.G. Bremerhaven and broken up.
41	ORMUZ II	14,588 8,082	550'-67.2'-35.1' 167.64-20.48-10.69m	--Launched 9 June 1914 as *Zeppelin*. --Yard No. 579. --Official No. 144399. --Builder, Bremer Vulkan, Vegesack, Germany for Norddeutscher Lloyd. --Twin screw, coal fired quadruple-expansion four-cylinder engines made and installed by the builder, 1,100nhp, 9,600ihp, 15.5 knots --Fitted with 99,710 cubic feet of refrigerated space.	308-nil-880	1921-27	14 / 13,333	--1919: War reparation ship handed over to the Allies after World War I, and used by the United States as a transport, handed over to Britain and the Shipping Controller with White Star Line as managers. --1921: Purchased by Orient Line in March and renamed *Ormuz*. --1921: First voyage to Australia as an Orient liner from London 12 November. --1926: Final voyage to Australia from London 27 November. --1927: Sold to Norddeutscher Lloyd, Bremen, Germany and renamed *Dresden*. --1934: On a cruise from Bremerhaven *Dresden* struck rocks off Norway and wrecked; three lives were lost. The wreck was sold to a firm at Stavanger.
42	ORAMA II	19,770 11,942	632'-75.2'-32.9' 192.63-22.92-10.02m	--Launched 20 May 1924. --Yard No. 598. --Official No. 146024. --Builder, Vickers Ltd, Barrow-in-Furness, England. --Twin screw, six Parsons-type geared steam turbines made and installed by the builder, 3,856nhp, 20,000shp, 20 knots. --Fitted with 187,325 cubic feet of refrigerated space.	As built First: 592 Third: 1,192 Crew: 440 From 1935 First: 484 Tourist: 498	1924-40	45 / 32,414	Steel, twin screw, five decks, seven holds, two funnels, two masts, straight stem, cruiser stern. --Fourteenth passenger steamship built for the Orient Steam Navigation Company's Australian service. --1924: Departed London on 15 November on maiden voyage to Australia. --1934: As an experiment her hull was painted in a corn colour, which was adopted by the Orient Line for ships commencing with *Orion*. --1939: Requisitioned as troop transport, World War II. --1940: In the North Sea on 8 June *Orama* encountered the German heavy cruiser *Admiral Hipper* and accompanying destroyers, which sank *Orama* by gunfire; twenty lives were lost and the surviving crew members were taken prisoner. During her war service, *Orama* sailed 37,046 miles and consumed 15,627 tons of fuel. In addition, she carried 6,755 troops.

Ref.	Ship	Tonnage Gross/Net	Dimensions Length, Beam, Depth Feet-Metres	Specifications As Built	Capacity As Built First-Second-Third-Crew (where known)	Australian Service	Voyages to Australia & Passengers Carried		Details
43	ORONSAY	20,001 11,441	633.6'-75.2'-33' 193.12-22.92-10.05m	--Launched 14 August 1924. --Yard No. 500. --Official No. 147948. --Builder, John Brown & Co., Ltd, Clydebank, Scotland. --Twin screw, six Brown-Curtis geared steam turbines made and installed by the builder, 3,811nhp, 20,000shp, 20 knots. --Fitted with 163,570 cubic feet of refrigerated space.	As built First: 596 Tourist: 1,184 Crew: 430 From 1935 First: 502 Tourist: 482	1925-42	41	27,670	Steel, twin screw, five decks, seven holds, two funnels, two masts, straight stem, cruiser stern. --Fifteenth passenger steamship built for the Orient Steam Navigation Company's Australian service. --1925: Departed London 7 February on maiden voyage to Australia. --1932: Made the Orient Lines' first Australian cruise from Sydney on 24 December for a six-day cruise to the French port of Noumea. --1938: One voyage from London was extended to New Zealand. --1940: World War II, requisitioned as troop transport. --1940: In the evacuation of France the Oronsay suffered severe damage from German bombers at Saint-Nazaire. --1942: Torpedoed and sunk on 9 October by Italian submarine Archimede off West Africa on a voyage from Cape Town to Britain. Six crew were lost. During her war service, Oronsay travelled 157,579 miles and consumed 64,947 tons of fuel. Carried 64,947 troops, 5,105 civilians and 635 prisoners-of-war.
44	OTRANTO II	20,032 12,031	632'-75.2'-32.9' 192.63-22.92-10.02m	--Launched 9 June 1925. --Yard No. 619. --Official No. 146025. --Builder, Vickers Ltd, Barrow-in-Furness, England. --Twin screw, six Parsons-type geared steam turbines made and installed by the builder, 3,722nhp, 20,000shp, 20 knots. --Fitted with 170,688 cubic feet of refrigerated space.	As built First: 572 Tourist: 1,168 Crew: 441 From 1935 First: 512 Tourist: 476 From 1949 Tourist: 1,412	1926-57	68	62,723	Steel, twin screw, five decks, seven holds, two funnels, two masts, straight stem, cruiser stern. --Sixteenth passenger steamship built for the Orient Steam Navigation Company's Australian service. --1926: Departed London 9 January on maiden voyage to Australia. --1926: Sustained severe bow damage when she collided with a cliff off Cape Grosso, Greece; repaired on return to Southampton. --1939: World War II, requisitioned as troop transport. --1948: Reconditioned after war service by Cammell Laird & Co., Birkenhead and returned to passenger service. --1949: Departed London 14 July on her first post-war commercial voyage to Australia. --1957: Final voyage to Australia from London 13 February. --1957: Sold in April to British Iron and Steel Corporation for scrap and broken up at Faslane.
45	ORFORD	19,941 12,027	632.2'-75.4'-33.1' 192.69-22.98-10.08m	--Launched 27 September 1927. --Yard No. 627. --Official No. 146026. --Builder, Vickers Ltd, Barrow-in-Furness, England. --Twin screw, six Parsons-type geared steam turbines made and installed by the builder, 3,825nhp, 20,000shp, 20 knots.	As built First: 520 Third: 1,162 Crew: 447 From 1935 First: 468 Tourist: 518	1928-40	24	12,848	Steel, twin screw, five decks, seven holds, two funnels, two masts, straight stem, cruiser stern. --Seventeenth passenger steamship built for the Orient Steam Navigation Company's Australian service. --1928: Departed London 13 October on her maiden Australian voyage. --1938/39: Two voyages from London were extended to New Zealand. --1939: Requisitioned for war service as troopship in World War II. --1940: On 1 June Orford was bombed by the Luftwaffe whilst at Marseilles, and was a total loss; fourteen lives were lost. Salvaged after the war, Orford was broken up at Savona. During her war service, Orford sailed 43,014 miles and consumed 16,544 tons of fuel. In addition she carried 18,580 troops.
46	ORONTES II	19,970 12,010	638.2'-75.3'-33.1' 194.52-22.95-10.08m	--Launched 26 February 1929. --Yard No. 637. --Official No. 146027. --Builder, Vickers-Armstrongs Ltd, Barrow-in-Furness, England. --Twin screw, six Parsons-type geared steam turbines made and installed by the builder, 3,825nhp, 20,000shp, 20 knots. --Fitted with 149,789 cubic feet of refrigerated space.	As built First: 508 Third: 1,112 From 1935 First: 463 Tourist: 528 From 1948 First: 502 Tourist: 618 From 1953 Tourist: 1,410	1929-62	71	67,017[1]	Steel, twin screw, five decks, seven holds, two funnels, two masts, straight stem, cruiser stern. --Eighteenth passenger steamship built for the Orient Steam Navigation Company's Australian service. --1929: Departed London 26 October on maiden Australian voyage. --1939: One voyage from London was extended to New Zealand. --1940: World War II, requisitioned as troop transport. --1947: Post-war refit by Thorneycroft & Co., Southampton. --1948: Departed London 17 June on first post-war commercial voyage to Australia. --1961: Final voyage to Australia from London 4 February. --1962: Sold for £282,000 for scrap to J.F. Ordaz y Compania, Madrid, Spain, for breaking up at Valencia.

1 The number of sailings, 71, and passengers carried, 67,017, relate to the Orient Line years prior to the merger with P&O in 1960. Orontes' final numbers after that merger are 77 sailings and 75,195 passengers carried.

Ref.	Ship	Tonnage Gross/Net	Dimensions Length, Beam, Depth Feet-Metres	Specifications As Built	Capacity As Built First-Second-Third- Crew (where known)	Australian Service	Voyages to Australia	& Passengers Carried	Details
47	ORION	23,371 14,032	640.3'-82.2'-33.7' 195.16-25.05-10.27m	--Launched 7 December 1934. --Yard No. 697. --Official No. 164493. --Builder, Vickers-Armstrongs Ltd, Barrow-in-Furness, England. --Twin screw, six Parsons-type geared steam turbines made and installed by the builder, 4,912nhp, 24,000shp, 20 knots. --Fitted with 209,215 cubic feet of refrigerated space.	As built First: 484 Tourist: 637 Crew: 470 From 1947 First: 550 Tourist: 700 From 1958 Cabin: 342 Tourist: 722 From 1961 Tourist: 1,691	1935-63	57	71,202[2]	Steel, twin screw, eight decks, six holds, one funnel, one mast, plated stem, cruiser stern. --Nineteenth steamship built for the Orient Steam Navigation Company's Australian service. --1934: The launching of Orion was unique in that her naming and releasing the baptismal wine was triggered by a radio transmission activated in Brisbane, Australia, by HRH the Duke of Gloucester. --1935: Departed London 28 September on her maiden Australia voyage. --1939: Requisitioned 26 August in anticipation for service as troop transport in World War II. --1941: On 2 September Orion was following close astern of the battleship HMS Revenge when the latter suddenly stopped and the Orion collided with her stern. Temporary repairs at Cape Town followed with major repairs at Singapore. --1943: Orion made two North Atlantic trooping voyages from New York to Britain carrying 7,000 troops on each voyage. --1946: Reconditioned after war service from May 1946 to January 1947 by Vickers-Armstrongs Ltd, Barrow-in-Furness, England. -- 1947: Departed London 25 February on first post-war commercial voyage to Australia. --1960: Transferred to P&O-Orient Lines. --1963: Final voyage to Australia from Southampton 28 February. --1963: Chartered as accommodation ship at the Hamburg International Horticultural Exhibition from May to September. --1963: Sold and broken up in 1963 at Antwerp, Jos Boles & Son SA.
48	ORCADES II	23,456 14,029	639.3'-82.2'-33.6' 194.86-25.05-10.24m	--Launched 1 December 1936. --Yard No. 712. --Official No. 165501. --Builder, Vickers-Armstrongs Ltd, Barrow-in-Furness. --Twin screw, six Parsons-type geared steam turbines made and installed by the builder, 4,912nhp, 24,000shp, 20 knots. --Fitted with 208,190 cubic feet of refrigerated space.	As built First: 463 Tourist: 605 Crew: 466	1937-42	8	5,060	Steel, twin screw, eight decks, six holds, one funnel, one mast, plated stem, cruiser stern. --Twentieth passenger steamship built for the Orient Steam Navigation Company's Australian service. --1937: Departed London 9 October on her maiden Australian voyage. --1939: Returned to builders in May for refit after engine problems. --1939: Requisitioned for service as troop transport in World War II. --1942: On 10 October Orcades was attacked and sunk by German Submarine U-172 in the South Atlantic. Forty-six lives were lost. During her war service, Orcades sailed a distance of 253,625 miles and consumed 76,661 tons of fuel. She carried 50,778 troops, 4,800 civilians and 1,000 prisoners-of-war.
49	ORCADES III	28,164 15,839	681.7'-90.8'-30.5' 207.78-27.67-9.16m	--Launched 14 October 1947. --Yard No. 950. --Official No. 182883. --Cost £3,245,000. --Builder, Vickers-Armstrongs Ltd, Barrow-in-Furness, England. --Twin screw, six Parsons-type geared steam turbines made and installed by the builder, 42,500shp, 22.5 knots. --Fitted with 238,460 cubic feet of refrigerated space.	As built First: 773 Tourist: 772 Crew: 617 From 1959 First: 631 Tourist: 734 From 1964 Tourist: 1,635	1948-73	35	45,395[3]	Steel, raked stem, nine decks, six holds, her signalling tripod mast, bridge and one vertical funnel almost amidships and in one structure. --Twenty-first passenger steamship built for the Orient Steam Navigation Company's Australian service. --1948: Departed London 14 December on maiden voyage to Australia. --1959: The Orcades was sent to Harland & Wolff, Belfast for a refit that included the installation of air-conditioning. The first Orient liner to be completely air-conditioned. --1960: Transferred to P&O-Orient Lines. --1962: Ownership was transferred to Peninsular and Oriental Steam Navigation Co. --1972: Final voyage to Australia from Southampton 21 February. --1973: Sold and broken up by Nan Feng Steel Enterprise Co., Ltd, at Kaohsiung, Taiwan.

2 The number of sailings, 57, and passengers carried, 71,202, relate to the Orient Line years prior to the merger with P&O in 1960. The final numbers for Orion after the merger are 68 sailings and 83,307 passengers.
3 The number of sailings, 35, and passengers carried, 45,395, relate to the Orient Line years prior to the merger with P&O in 1960. The final numbers of Orcades after the merger are 70 sailings and 90,265 passengers.

Ref.	Ship	Tonnage Gross/Net	Dimensions Length, Beam, Depth Feet-Metres	Specifications As Built	Capacity As Built First-Second-Third-Crew (where known)	Australian Service	Voyages to Australia	& Passengers Carried	Details
50	ORONSAY II	27,632 15,122	681.7bp'-90.1'-30.5' 207.78-27.46-9.29m	--Launched 30 June 1950. --Yard No. 976. --Official No. 184415. --Signal Letters GCNB. --Cost, £4,228,000. --Builder Vickers-Armstrongs Ltd, Barrow-in-Furness, England. --Twin screw, six Pametrada-type geared steam turbines made and installed by the builder, 42,500shp, 22.5 knots. --Speed on trials 25.23 knots. --Fitted with 222,990 cubic feet of refrigerated space.	As built First: 668 Tourist: 833 Crew: 622 From 1972 Tourist: 1,400 Crew: 600+	1951-75	27	37,466[4]	Steel, raked stem, nine decks, six holds, her signalling mast, bridge and one funnel almost amidships and in one structure. --Twenty-second passenger steamship built for the Orient Steam Navigation Company's Australian service. --1950: Damaged by fire whilst being fitted out. --1951: Departed London 16 May on maiden voyage to Australia. --1954: Inaugurated the Orient Line's trans-Pacific service from Sydney 1 January to North America. --1959: Oronsay was sent to Harland & Wolff, Liverpool for a refit that included the installation of air-conditioning. --1960: Transferred to P&O-Orient Lines. --1962: Ownership transferred to Peninsular and Oriental Steam Navigation Co. --1975: Final voyage to Australia. --1975: Sold and broken up by Nan Feng Steel Enterprise Co., Ltd, at Kaohsiung, Taiwan.
51	ORSOVA II	28,790 15,882	691'-90.6'-31' 210.61-27.61-9.45m	--Launched 14 May 1953. --Yard No. 1021. --Official No. 186017. --Cost £5,776,000. --Builder, Vickers-Armstrongs Ltd, Barrow-in-Furness. --Twin screw, six Pametrada-type geared steam turbines made and installed by the builder, 42,500shp, 22.5 knots. --Fitted with 313,350 cubic feet of refrigerated space.	As built First: 685 Tourist: 813 Crew: 620+	1954-74	18	23,445[5]	Steel, curved-swan like bow, nine decks, six holds, bridge and one funnel almost amidships and in one structure. --Twenty-third passenger steamship built for the Orient Steam Navigation Company's Australian service. --1954: Departed London 17 March on maiden voyage to Australia. --1960: Orsova was sent to Vickers-Armstrongs (Shipbuilders) Ltd, Newcastle-upon-Tyne, for a refit that included the installation of air-conditioning. --1960: Transferred to P&O-Orient Lines. --1965: Ownership transferred to Peninsular and Oriental Steam Navigation Co. --1974: Sold and broken up by Nan Feng Steel Enterprise Co., Ltd, at Kaohsiung, Taiwan.
52	ORIANA	41,915 22,354	740'-97.2'-32' 225.55-29.62-9.75m	--Launched 3 November 1959. --Yard No. 1061. --Official No. 301235. --Builder, Vickers-Armstrongs Ltd, Barrow-in-Furness. --Twin screw, six Pametrada-type geared steam turbines made and installed by the builder, 80,000shp, 27.5 knots. --Fitted with 52,530 cubic feet of refrigerated space.	As built First: 685 Tourist: 1,496 From 1973 One Class: 1,677	1960-86	51	78,235	--Twenty-fourth passenger steamship built for the Orient Steam Navigation Company's Australian service. --1960: Departed Southampton 3 December on maiden voyage to Australia; reached Sydney from Southampton in twenty-seven days. --1962: Suffered bow damage when collided with the aircraft carrier USS Kearsage near Long Beach, California. --1965: Ownership transferred to Peninsular and Oriental Steam Navigation Co. --1986: Sold to Daiwa House, Japan, for use as floating cultural attraction. --1995: Sold to Chinese interests at Qinhuangdao. --1998: Sold to Shanghai Oriana Entertainment Co. and taken to Shanghai. --2000: Sold at auction. --2002: Towed to Dalian, China, as floating tourist attraction. --2004: Was damaged during a storm and partly sank, condemned and subsequently broken up.

4 The number of sailings, 27 and passengers carried, 37,466 relate to the Orient Line years prior to the merger with P&O in 1960. The final numbers for Oronsay after that merger are 64 sailings and 76,035 passengers.
5 The number of sailings, 18 and passengers carried, 23,445 relate to the Orient Line years prior to the merger with P&O in 1960. The final numbers for Orsova after the merger are 50 sailings and 59,459 passengers.

APPENDIX 3

Orient Steam Navigation Company

Ships managed by the Orient Line during and after World War I and World War II on behalf of the Ministry of War Transport and the Shipping Controller. (Henderson & Cremer Collection)

Ship	Tons Gross Net	Measurement Imperial (feet) Metric	Machinery	Details
Huntsgreen	9,060 5,148	481'oa-57.4'-35.5' 145.8-17.3-10.8m	--Builder, F. Schichau, Danzig. --Twin screw, 8-cylinder quadruple-expansion engines by the builder, 820nhp, 14.5 knots.	--1907: Launched on 9 November for the Norddeutscher Lloyd Company as the *Derfflinger* for their Far East service. --1914: Seized off Port Said on 13 October by HMS *Foxhound*, renamed *Huntsgreen*, she was then managed by F. Green & Co., before passing to Union-Castle Steamship Co., and finally to the Orient Steam Navigation Co., in 1919. --1921: Released from Orient Line management, the *Huntsgreen* was sold before returning to her original owners in 1923 and reverting to the name *Derfflinger*.
Rio Negro	4,556 2,879	361.2'-46.7'-26.1' 114.6oa-14.3-7.95m	--Builder, Joh. C. Tecklenborg, A.G. Geestemünde. --Single screw, triple-expansion engine by the builder, 2,200hp, 11 knots.	--1905: Launched on 20 February for the Hamburg-Südamerikanischen Dampfschifffahrts-Gesellschaft for their Hamburg to Brazil service. --1914: Requisitioned by Imperial German Navy as support and supply ship. --1919: As war reparation, taken over by The Shipping Controller, London and put under the management of the Orient Line. --1921: Sold to Ellerman Lines, Liverpool and renamed *City of Palermo*. --1933: Sold and broken up in Italy.
Rio Pardo	4,588	361.1'-46.7'-26.1' 114.6oa-14.3-7.95m	--Builder, Joh C. Tecklenborg, A.G. Geestemünde. --Single screw, triple-expansion engine by the builder, 2,200hp, 11 knots.	--1905: Launched on 20 May for the Hamburg-Südamerikanischen Dampfschifffahrts-Gesellschaft for their Hamburg to Brazil service. --1919: As war reparation, taken over by The Shipping Controller, London then passed to Orient Line management. --1920: Sold to Ellerman Lines, Liverpool and renamed *City of Alexandria*. --1936: Sold and broken up in Italy.
Friedrichsruhe	8,332	469.2'-55.1'-29.7' 143-16.8-9.1m	--Builder, Fairfield Shipbuilding and Engineering Company, Glasgow. --Twin screw, quadruple-expansion engines.	--1905: Launched 22 March for the Hamburg-Amerika Line as the *Fürst Bismarck* for their New York service. --1914: Renamed *Friedrichsruhe*. --1919: As war reparation, taken over by The Shipping Controller, then passed to Orient Line management. --1922: Released from Orient Line management.
Cordoba	4,889	376.5'bp-46.3'-30.2' 114.8-14.1-9.2m	--Builder, Reihherstieg Schiffswerfte & Machinenfabrik, A.G. Hamburg. --Single screw, quadruple-expansion engine, 1,825ihp, 10.5 knots.	--1895: Launched for the Hamburg-Südamerikanischen Dampfschifffahrts-Gesellschaft. --1919: As war reparation, taken over by The Shipping Controller, London, then passed to Orient Line management.

Ship	Tons Gross Net	Measurement Imperial (feet) Metric	Machinery	Details
Christiaan Huygens	16,287	551.4'-68.8'-36.2' 167.6bp-20.8-12.1m	--Builder, N. v. Nederlandsche Shipbuilding Co., Amsterdam, Netherlands. --Twin screw, 2-stroke single acting, 20 cylinders, Sulzer engines, 11,600bhp, 16.5 knots.	--1927: Launched 28 September for Stoomvaart Maatschappij Nederland for their East Indies service. --1939: On the outbreak of World War II the Christiaan Huygens was chartered to the British Ministry of War Transport as a troopship and placed under the management of the Orient Line. --1945: Released from Orient Line management; however, on 28 August, the Christiaan Huygens struck a mine in the River Scheldt and was subsequently lost.
Johan van Oldenbarneveldt	20,314	587'-75'-36.1' 178.9-22.8-11.9m	--Builder, Nederlandse Scheepsbouw Maatschappij, Amsterdam. --Twin screw, Sulzer diesel engines, 19 knots.	--1929: Launched 3 August for Stoomvaart Maatschappij Nederland for their East Indies Round World service. --1940: Chartered in July to the British Ministry of War Transport as a troopship under the management of the Orient Line. --1946: Released from Orient Line management and returned to owners.
Marnix Van St Aldegonde	19,355	580'-74.5'-39.3' 176.79-22.70-11.98m	--Builder, N. v. Nederlandsche Shipbuilding Co., Amsterdam, Netherlands. --Twin screw, two 10-cylinder Scheldt-Sulzer diesel engines, 17 knots.	--1929: Launched 21 December for Stoomvaart Maatschappij Nederland for their East Indies and associated services. --1941: Chartered in May to the British Ministry of War Transport as a troopship under the management of the Orient Line. --1943: In convoy she was torpedoed by German aircraft when off North Africa; taken in tow, but sank a day later.
Johan De Witt	10,474	482.2'-59.2'-34.8' 159.4oa-18-10.6m	--Builder, Nederlandse Scheepsbouw Maatschappij, Amsterdam. --Twin screw, triple-expansion engines by Nederlandsche Factory of tools & Railway equipment, Amsterdam, 7,000ihp, 16.5 knots.	--1919: Launched 2 May for Stoomvaart Maatschappij Nederland for their East Indies service. --1940: Chartered in July to the British Ministry of War Transport as a troopship under the management of the Orient Line. --1946: Released from Orient Line management and returned to owners.
Samkansa	7,218	441.05'oa-57.1'-37.3' 134.4-17.3-11.4m	--Builder, Bethlehem Shipyard Inc., Baltimore. USA. --Single screw, triple-expansion three-cylinder engine by Harrisburg Machinery Corp., 2,500ihp, 11 knots.	--1943: Launched on 25 September as Nikola Tesla, renamed Samkansa and chartered to British Ministry of War Transport under the management of the Orient Line. --1947: Orient Line management ceased.
Sameveron	7,220	441.05'oa-57.1'-37.3' 134.4-17.3-11.4m	--Builder, Bethlehem Shipyard Inc., Baltimore, USA. --Single screw, triple-expansion three-cylinder engine by General Machinery Corp., Hamilton, Ohio.	--1944: Launched on 7 January for the United States War Administration and chartered to the British Ministry of War Transport under the management of the Orient Line. --1947: Orient Line management ceased.
Empire Orwell	16,662	574.40'a-72.2'-44.5' 175-22-13.5m	--Builder, Blohm & Voss, Hamburg, Germany. --Twin screw, six geared steam turbines built by the builder, 14,000shp, 4,050nhp, 18 knots.	--1936: Launched 16 July as Pretoria for Deutsch Ost-Afrika Linie, of Hamburg, for their African service. --1945: As war reparation, taken over and passed to Ministry of Transport, London. Refitted at Newcastle, renamed Empire Doon then passed to Orient Line management. --1947–49: Converted to troopship by Thornycroft and Co., Ltd, of Southampton. Renamed Empire Orwell in 1948. --1957: Orient Line management ceased.

BIBLIOGRAPHY

Original Orient Line Documents

Many details in this book are verified in the Orient Steam Navigation Co. minutes. The minutes form part of the Henderson & Cremer collection and are one of the last surviving copies known to exist in the world.

P.S.N. Co. Documents

Pacific Steam Navigation Company papers, Minute Book 1.1.8. Merseyside Maritime Museum.

Newspapers – Accessed via Trove at www.trove.nla.gov.au

Adelaide Observer, Adelaide, 19 March 1887, *Arrival of the Orient Steam Ship Ormuz.*
Albany Advertiser, Albany, 29 November 1922, *The Albany Advertiser.*
Albany Advertiser, Albany, 7 December 1929, *Luxury Liner: Orient Line's New 'Orontes'.*
Albury Banner and Wodonga Express, Albany, 23 September 1921, *Navigation Act.*
Albury Banner and Wodonga Express, Albany, 2 October 1936, *Ormonde Fire Extinguished.*
Australian Town and Country Journal, Sydney, 27 October 1883, *The Orient Mail Contract.*
Bendigo Advertiser, Bendigo, 25 October 1917, *Steamer Orama Sunk.*
Daily Commercial News and Shipping List, 19 December 1931, *Orient Liner Ormonde.*
Daily Commercial News and Shipping List, 13 November 1935, *Orient Chairman.*
Daily Commercial News and Shipping List, 3 December 1942, *Oronsay Sunk.*
Daily Commercial News and Shipping List, 15 April 1953, *Oronsay for Transpacific Service.*
Daily Mercury, Mackay, 3 January 1945, *1,040 Rescued when Orcades was Sunk.*
Daily Telegraph, Launceston, 28 February 1925, *Orient Steam Navigation Company.*
Eastern Districts Chronicle, York, 14 July 1906, *Saturday, July 14, 1906.*
Evening Journal, Adelaide, 25 November 1869, *Shipping News – Miscellaneous.*
Evening Journal, Adelaide, 18 March 1880, *'Cricket'.*
Horsham Times, Victoria, 14 November 1922, *Reasonless Strikes.*
Mount Alexander Mail, Mount Alexander, 24 December 1908, *Launch of a Liner for the Australian Mail Service.*
Mudgee Guardian and North-Western Representative, New South Wales, 29 November 1928, *Orford Arrives in Sydney.*
Newcastle Morning Herald, Newcastle, 19 February 1932, *The Orford and Bridge Opening.*
News, Adelaide, 27 November 1928, *Epic of Sea.*

Northern Star, Lismore, 4 May 1887, *Raising the Austral.*
Northern Star, Lismore, 15 January 1949, *Orcades in Sydney Records Topple on Maiden Voyage.*
Observer, Adelaide, 9 November 1907, *English Mail Contract.*
Portland Guardian, Victoria, 19 February 1945, *The Sinking of the 'Orcades' and 'Oronsay'.*
South Australian Chronicle & Weekly Mail, Adelaide, 5 June 1880, *The Australian Eleven.*
The Advertiser, Adelaide, 10 February 1893, *The Orient Line.*
The Age, Melbourne, 22 January 1906, *Melbourne Monday.*
The Argus, Melbourne, 6 May 1882, *The SS Orient.*
The Argus, Melbourne, 31 October 1882, *The SS Austral.*
The Argus, Melbourne, 22 February 1927, *Sir Frederick Green.*
The Argus, Melbourne, 17 April 1954, *Miss Orsova Met her New Namesake.*
The Argus, Melbourne, 26 May 1956, *On the Waterfront.*
The Argus, Melbourne, 27 October 1956, *Pilot to be Charged.*
The Ballarat Courier, Ballarat, 25 October 1917, *Steamer Orama Sunk (Reuters).*
The Bathurst Times, NSW, 27 July 1917, *Liner Otway Sunk.*
The Brisbane Courier, Brisbane, 15 November 1922, *Orient Trouble.*
The Brisbane Courier, Brisbane, 26 December 1927, *To-days News in Brief.*
The Canberra Times, Canberra, 31 December 1960, *Thousands Greet New Liner.*
The Canberra Times, Canberra, 17 April 1961, *Pilgrims Revisit Tobruk.*
The Canberra Times, Canberra, 18 July 1967, *Fire Aboard Oronsay.*
The Canberra Times, Canberra, 26 December 1993, *New Oriana Aiming for 1995 Launch.*
The Daily News, Perth, 28 October 1935, Orion Here Tomorrow.
The Daily Telegraph, Sydney, 13 July 1918, Was the Omrah Sunk? No Official Information.
The Evening News, Sydney, 7 September 1883, *The Orient Mail Contract.*
The Express and Telegraph, Adelaide, 28 February 1899, *The New Orient Liner Omrah.*
The Queenslander, Brisbane, 27 February 1886, *New Orient Steamers.*
The Register, Adelaide, 14 October 1918, *Transport Otranto Sunk.*
The South Australian Register, Adelaide, 15 October 1884, *An Orient Mail Contract.*
The Sun, Sydney, 27 March 1941, *Orama's Crew Interned.*
The Sun, Sydney, 10 November 1943, *Orama Men Released.*
The Swan Express, 15 October 1936, *Orient Line Tourist Class.*
The Sydney Mail and New South Wales Advertisers, Sydney, 8 July 1882, *The Orient Company's Steamship Austral.*
The Sydney Morning Herald, Sydney, 13 March 1883, *The Raising of the SS Austral.*
The Sydney Morning Herald, Sydney, 30 May 1907, *Orient Company and the Mail Contract.*
The Sydney Morning Herald, Sydney, 28 July 1917, *Orient Line Officers Honoured.*
The Sydney Morning Herald, Sydney, 23 January 1954, *Pacific Ship Service.*
The Western Herald, Bourke, 20 January 1961, *A Bank Goes to Sea.*
Tweed Daily, Murwilumbah, 6 August 1945, *Orontes Returns to Australia.*
Wellington Times, New South Wales, 30 September 1954, *Orient Line Commodore Retired.*
Western Mail, Perth, 20 March 1924, *An Eventful Voyage.*

Newspapers

The Times of London, London, 29 June 1880, *The Electrical Light A Highly Successful Application*.
The Times of London, London, 13 February 1878, *Money Markets and City Intelligence*.

Websites

Australian National Maritime Museum, *The Opulent Ship with a Royal Connection* posted 27 July 2013 by Kim Tao, anmm.blog/tag/royal-tour (accessed November 2017).

AWA Technology Services, www.awa.com.au/about-us/our-history/ (accessed November 2017)

Blue Star Line Website, *Tuscan Star* Article, www.bluestarline.org/tuscan1.html.

Cunard Line Website (archived at Way Back Machine), *Lancastria*, Cunard Heritage, web.archive. org/web/20061024105800/www.cunardline.com/AboutCunard/default.asp?Active=Heritage& Sub=GetShip&ShipID=91 (archived on 24 October 2006 and accessed December 2017).

Financial Review, *Why the Great Australian Property Crash of 1891 Could Happen Again,* by Stewart Oldfield, 6 January 2016 www.afr.com/personal-finance/the-great-australian-property-crash-of-1891-why-it-could-happen-again-20151207-glh724 (accessed November 2017).

How Stat: The Cricket Statistics, www.howstat.com (accessed December 2017).

Mariners, Liberty Ships 'S', www.mariners-l.co.uk/LibShipsS.html (accessed October 2017).

NZ Maritime, The Orient Liner SS Oriana, www.nzmaritime.co.nz/oriana.htm (accessed December 2017).

Passengers in History, Initiative of the South Australian Maritime Museum, http://www. passengersinhistory.sa.gov.au (accessed July 2018).

P&O Heritage, Orontes 1929, www.poheritage.com/Upload/Mimsy/Media/ factsheet/94099ORONTES-1929pdf.pdf (accessed December 2017).

SS Maritime, SS *Oriana* to the Breakers, www.ssmaritime.com/oriana-1.htm (accessed December 2017).

Seadogs Reunited, *Oriana* Fire, www.seadogs-reunited.com/Oriana.htm (accessed December 2017).

The Ships List, www.theshipslist.com (accessed November 2017).

The Great Ocean Liners, *Oriana* 1960–2005, The Great Ocean Liners, www.thegreatoceanliners. com/oriana.html (accessed December 2017).

Government-Issued Documents

Australian War Memorial, *Prime Minister Robert G. Menzies Wartime Broadcast*, Australian War Memorial, www.awm.gov.au/articles/encyclopedia/prime_ministers/menzies (retrieved 15 December 2017).

National Archives and Records Administration, *American Reports on Aid to Allies (ETC)*, archive.org/details/gov.archives.arc.38937 (retrieved 13 December 2017).

New Zealand History, *New Zealand Declares War on Germany*, nzhistory.govt.nz/new-zealand-declares-war-on-germany (retrieved 16 December 2017).

Parliament of Australia, *To the Last Man: Australia's Entry to War in 1914,* by Curtis Jonathan, www.aph.gov.au/About_Parliament/Parliamentary_Departments/Parliamentary_Library/pubs/rp/rp1415/AustToWar1914 (retrieved 13 December 2017).

Proceedings of the Strathleven Centenary Symposium on Refrigeration. Held on 26 and 27 February 1980, CSIRO Alumni, c.ymcdn.com/sites/www.csiroalumni.org.au/resource/collection/562A1129-C908-425D-9FE0-FBA409DBCAC0/Vol_40_No_3_&_4_1980a.pdf (retrieved 3 January 2018).

Royal Commission on the Butter Industry Progress Report on Open Markets, Grading, Temperatures, Ocean Freights, Butter for Export, Home Separator, Treatment of Cream, Brands, Cool Stores and Trucks; with Summary of Recommendations and Appendix, Victoria 1904, www.parliament.vic.gov.au (retrieved 2 December 2017).

Books

Bertke, D., Kindell, D., and Smith, G., (2009) *World War II Sea War (Volume 2).* Bertke Publications.

Frame, C., and Cross, R., (2015) *175 Years of Cunard.* The History Press.

Henderson, R., Cremer, D., Frame, C., and Cross, R., (2014) *A Photographic History of P&O Cruises.* The History Press.

McCart, N., (1987) *Passenger ships of the Orient Line.* Patrick Stephens.

Miller, W.H. (1995) *Pictorial Encyclopaedia of Ocean Liners*, 1860–1994. Dover.

Morris, C.F. (1980) *Origins, Orient and Oriana.* Teredo Books.

Poole, S., and Sassoli-Walker, A., (2011) *P&O Cruises: Celebrating 175 Years of Heritage.* Amberley.

Correspondence

Letter from the Orient Line to *The Times of London*, dated May 1880.

Personal Conversations

Rob Henderson conversations with: Alan Armour, Ivor Geddes, Kenneth Anderson and the countless Orient Line captains, officers and staff with whom I have had so many wonderful conversations.
Rob Henderson, Chris Frame, Rachelle Cross and Doug Cremer conversations with Commodore Christopher Rynd about Orient Line and P&O; 2012–18.
Rob Henderson conversations with Bob (Robert) McLaughlin, various years.

State Library of Victoria Pictures Collection References

H91.325/436	H91.325/1588
H91.250/722	H81.325/436
H91.108/1597	H81.85/98
H91.325/448	H82.166/27
H91. 325/553	H82.166/39
H91.325/446	H82.166/123
H91.325/459	

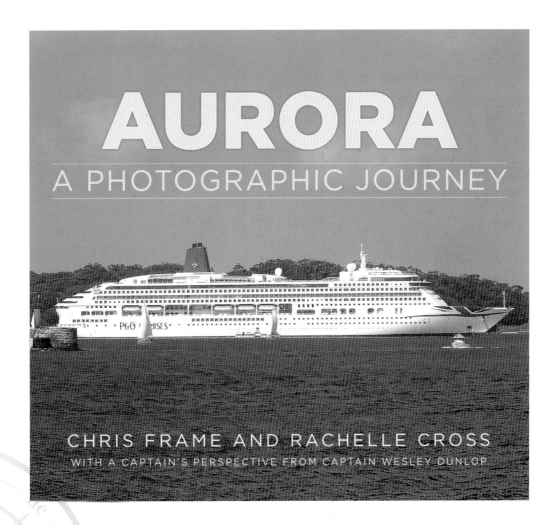

AURORA
A PHOTOGRAPHIC JOURNEY

CHRIS FRAME AND RACHELLE CROSS

WITH A CAPTAIN'S PERSPECTIVE FROM CAPTAIN WESLEY DUNLOP

978 0 7509 8582 6

The History Press — The destination for history — www.thehistorypress.co.uk

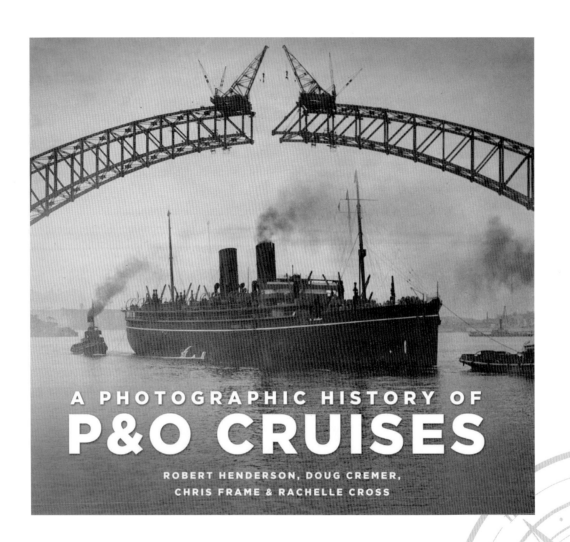

A PHOTOGRAPHIC HISTORY OF
P&O CRUISES

ROBERT HENDERSON, DOUG CREMER,
CHRIS FRAME & RACHELLE CROSS

978 0 7524 8901 8